Contents

To all the men and women of the U.S. armed services who fly "the dull, the dirty, and the dangerous" missions for which unmanned air vehicles and unmanned *combat* air vehicles are the ideal weapon, and often the *only* weapon for the task.

"Innovative doctrine and high-tech weaponry can shape and then dominate an unconventional conflict. Our commanders are gaining a real-time picture of the entire battlefield, and are able to get targeting information from sensor to shooter almost instantly. . . . Before the war, the Predator UAV had skeptics because it did not fit the old ways. Now it is clear the military does not have enough unmanned vehicles."

—President George W. Bush
Charleston, South Carolina
(December 11, 2001)

"We've been watching for where the bad guys hide, move or want to hide. . . . If we're carrying Hellfire missiles, we can take care of a target ourselves."

—Captain Traz Trzaskoma, U.S. Air Force Predator pilot
(Somewhere in Iraq, April 2003)

"We're at a threshold of something very, very exciting and very, very new with unmanned aerial vehicles, whether they are unmanned combat aerial vehicles or reconnaissance UAVs."

—Lieutenant General Michael Moseley
Commander, U.S. Central Command Air Forces
(April 5, 2003, the 18th day of Gulf War II)

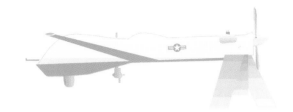

Acknowledgments

The author wishes to thank the following people who helped with supplying images and information for this book: Craig Ballard of Pioneer UAV, Inc.; Cynthia Curiel of Northrop Grumman Corporation; Mike Lombardi and Larry Merritt of the Boeing Archives; Rebe Philip of General Atomics Aeronautical Systems; Eric Schulzinger of Lockheed Martin Multimedia Communications; Erik Simonsen of Boeing Air Force Systems; and Al Lloyd, who shared photographs from his Firebee collection.

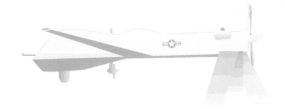

Prologue

On November 4, 2002, a sport-utility vehicle bounced along a country road that winds through the monotonous gray gravel hills of the Marib region, about 100 miles east of Sanaa, the capital of Yemen. Among the six men inside were Qaed Senyan al-Harthi and Kamal Derwish, a pair of Yemenis who were members of Osama bin Laden's al-Qaeda terrorist gang. Al-Harthi, who also went by the street name "Abu Ali," was bin Laden's "capo" for Yemen. He was also one of the schemers who had planned the suicide attack that had damaged the USS *Cole* in Yemen 25 months earlier, killing 17 Americans. Derwish, a Yemeni who had assumed the pseudonym "Ahmed Hijazi," immigrated to the United States and became a U.S. citizen. In turn, he headed an al-Qaeda "sleeper cell" in Lackawanna, New York.

As they drove across the Marib desert, the six al-Qaeda probably chatted about their jihad against the United States. They may also have been discussing the five members of Derwish's gang—all Yemenis who had taken American citizenship—who had been busted in Lackawanna by the FBI two weeks earlier. Al-Harthi and Derwish knew that they too were wanted by the FBI, but they were possibly more concerned that they were also being tracked by the Yemeni government, which was especially angry with al-Harthi's al-Qaeda gang after a shootout in late 2001 that had left more than a dozen Yemeni soldiers dead.

Occasionally, one of the men in the SUV would excuse himself to make a quick cell-phone call, possibly to Muhammad Hamdi al-Ahdal, another Yemeni who had been involved in the attack on the USS *Cole*—or to Jaber Elbaneh, another member of Derwish's sleeper cell who had also escaped to Yemen when things had gotten hot in Lackawanna.

About 10,000 feet above the gangsters, traveling scarcely faster than their sport utility vehicle, was a gangly, pale-colored airplane. Through a television link in this unmanned craft, an American sitting in a control center about 350 miles away in Djibouti had been watching the SUV for about an hour.

Suddenly a flash of fire erupted on the wing of the lumbering airplane. A contrail streaked toward the desert floor. Before they had a chance to ponder their wasted martyrdom, the six gangsters felt a terrible explosion jolt the SUV, and they were instantly engulfed in a furiously burning ball of unleaded gasoline. They didn't have even a moment to think about the irony of all those civilians who had burned to death in those other high-octane balls of fire in the buildings that al-Qaeda had targeted on September 11, 2001.

Historians would liken the November 4, 2002, strike to that of April 18, 1943, when a U.S. Army Air Forces P-38 Lightning piloted by Captain Thomas G. Lanphier Jr. shot down an Imperial Japanese Navy G4M bomber over Bougainville in the South Pacific. Riding as a passenger in that G4M had been Admiral Isoroku Yamamoto, commander in chief of the Imperial Navy—and the architect of the attack on Pearl Harbor.

When that MQ-1B Predator unmanned aerial vehicle (UAV) took out the al-Qaeda SUV with an AGM-114 Hellfire air-attack missile on that November day, it had been a small but important turning point in military history. It was not so much that terrorist masterminds were no longer available to engage in deadly mischief: it was that unmanned aerial platforms were making the transition from the passive to the active. Long used for aerial reconnaissance, UAVs were now on the offensive.

The November 4, 2002, attack was not the first use of a UAV in combat. Predators had been armed with Hellfires a year earlier during the war in Afghanistan, and they had played a role in taking out Muhammad Atef, a principal bin Laden henchman, in November 2001. The 2002 attack was, however, the first widely publicized successful attack on a "high value" target by a Predator operating alone. It is also the first time that an armed Predator is known to have struck an operational target outside the Afghan Theater.

The armed Predator was the first American UAV to go on the offensive in live combat, but the U.S. Defense Department had been working on the concept of a whole new family of unmanned combat aerial vehicles (UCAVs) since the mid-1990s. The original concept was that the UCAVs would not be operational until the end of the first decade of the new century. Then came the September 11, 2001, attacks, and the U.S. armed forces found themselves in Afghanistan chasing exactly the kinds of targets that called out for a weapons system just like an armed Predator. Sooner than expected, the drones were on the attack.

One weapons pylon is ominously empty on this General Atomics MQ-1 Predator, seen here forward-deployed to an undisclosed location in the Middle East. Parked in its temporary shelter, this 15th Expeditionary Reconnaissance Squadron bird of prey has been out hunting tonight. The eyes of its Lynx side aperture radar in the 14-inch Skyball gimbal have *seen*, and the talons of the AGM-114 Hellfire missile on the starboard talon have *struck*. *U.S. Air Force Captain John Sheets*

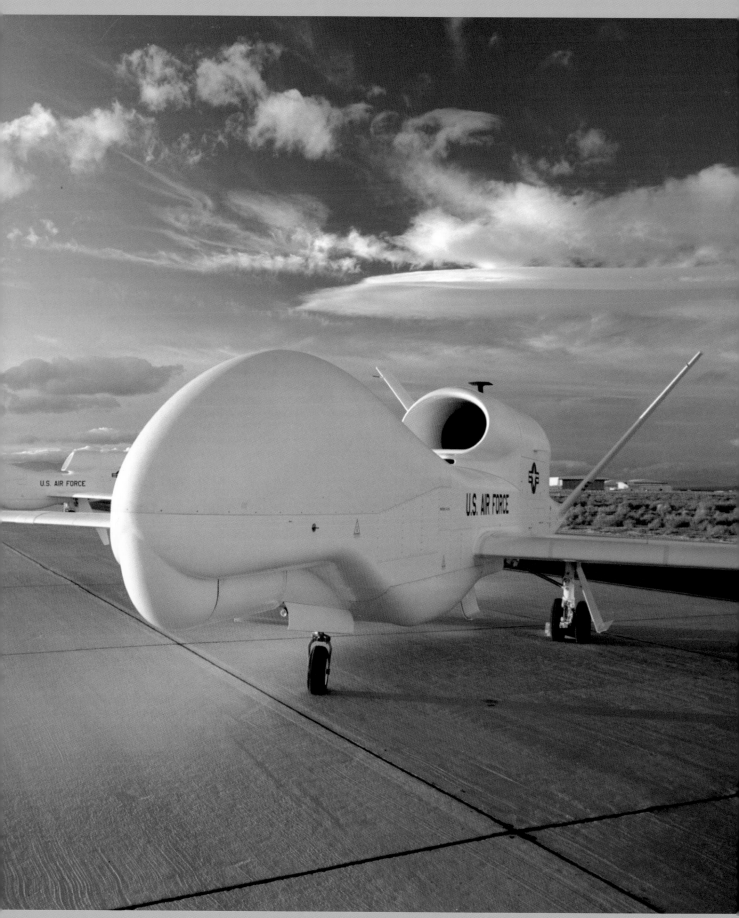

The World of the Unmanned Combat Aerial Vehicle

Many books have begun with the phrase "It used to be science fiction, but now it's science *fact*." Nowhere in the world of today's military technology is this transition from fiction to fact more astounding than in the dark world of autonomous unmanned aerial combat vehicles.

Since the United States began using them in the global war on terrorism, the exploits of armed Predators have piqued the curiosity of the public and excited those interested in military technology. Even as the Predators were grabbing headlines, many people in the armed forces and aerospace industry were hard at work defining a new generation of unmanned aircraft that would be designed from the ground up as unmanned combat aerial vehicles.

These UCAVs would be designed to perform a whole spectrum of attack missions, including missions that were once flown only by aircraft with a pilot aboard—and *especially* missions where those

LEFT: Dawn has arrived, and these Hawks are ready to fly. Their high-altitude missions may keep these Northrop Grumman RQ-4A Global Hawks aloft through another sunrise or two. Their long endurance could take them halfway around the world before they rest and refuel. When the flight crew resides on the ground, fatigue is no longer an impediment to long-distance missions. *Northrop Grumman*

intelligent human pilots were in extraordinary danger of being killed. The U.S. military hates to lose aircraft—but it *really* doesn't like to lose pilots.

In the words of Rich Alldredge, the UCAV program manager for Boeing's Phantom Works, "Removing the pilot eliminates the need for pilot systems and interfaces, and allows for a smaller, simpler aircraft. No sorties are required for pilot training, and UCAVs can be placed in flight-ready storage for years, eliminating consumables, maintenance, and personnel requirements."

These qualities also simplify the decision to launch high-risk attacks. As Major Rob Vanderberry of the U.S. Air Force's Air Combat Command put it, "These aircraft will allow Air Force leaders to breathe easier when making a combat decision. What UCAV lets us do is attack a target without the concern of losing a pilot, or having someone become a prisoner of war."

While UAVs and UCAVs are not designed to be expendable, meaning that the armed services don't intend to lose them every time they're sent on a mission, they are, in Defense Department parlance, "attritable." This means that a commander can *afford* to lose one through attrition, especially when the alternative is the loss of a manned aircraft or an aircrew.

The Boeing X-45A, seen here undergoing an engine checkout during the spring of 2001 at the Dryden Flight Research Center, is the first prototype of an unmanned combat air vehicle that was built from the ground up as a warplane without a pilot aboard. *DARPA*

A twenty-first-century naval unmanned combat air vehicle (UCAV-N) touches down on the deck of an aircraft carrier. The configuration seen here combines features of the "kite" aerodynamic shape that Northrop Grumman successfully demonstrated with its X-47A Pegasus experimental UAV with a "flying wing." This enables long endurance and high survivability as well as excellent carrier launch and recovery flying qualities. *Northrop Grumman Media Relations*

Unmanned aerial vehicles don't put lives at risk, and that has led to the common misconception that they are cheap. They are generally less expensive than manned aircraft, but they are not cheap enough to be disposable. The costs of the larger UAVs in service around the turn of the century ranged from around a half-million dollars to nearly the equivalent of manned aircraft prices. The payloads, sensors, airframes, and control and communication networks that are combined to provide the necessary capability are not inexpensive.

When people in the UAV and UCAV world speak of what types of missions their aircraft are right for, the answer is "the dull, the dirty, and the dangerous": in other words, long, dull, repetitive reconnaissance missions; sorties into a battlefield environment made "dirty" by chemical or biological weapons; or attacks against targets that are very dangerous for human pilots. The latter includes the suppression of enemy air defenses (SEAD) missions, in which attack aircraft are exposed to high volumes of fire from antiaircraft artillery (AAA) and surface-to-air missiles (SAMs). In 2001–2003 actions in Afghanistan and Iraq, such missions were flown by Air Force F-16s and U.S. Navy/U.S. Marine Corps F/A-18s supported by EA-6B electronic warfare aircraft that were tasked with jamming enemy defensive radar. All of these have human crews who risk their lives. In the UCAV future, only the airplanes would be at risk in SEAD missions.

While UAV technology is being developed in many countries, this book will focus primarily on American programs. This is not because important UAVs are not being developed elsewhere, but because the U.S. armed services have committed to a long-term and comprehensive development of families of UAVs and UCAVs that operate on many tiers of capability and are tailored for a broad spectrum of missions. This book is the story of the evolution of the unarmed UAVs, of how UAVs have morphed into UCAVs, and how both UAVs and UCAVs will develop in the twenty-first century.

Cruise Missiles

These are winged aircraft without a pilot aboard that are designed to be used as projectiles. Operationally, they are like a ballistic missile or an artillery shell. They fly like an airplane, but their mission is complete when they are destroyed upon impact with their targets. Current examples include the Raytheon BGM-109 Tomahawk, the McDonnell

WHAT ARE UNMANNED AERIAL VEHICLES?

There are three types of unmanned aircraft with military applications. Throughout history, most—but not all—have been operated through remote control by a pilot on the ground or in another airplane. Such vehicles differ from ballistic missiles—which are essentially guided artillery shells—in that they have wings and fly like airplanes with a crew aboard. Indeed, they are airplanes. Such aircraft are often known generically as "drones" because they are directed by an external source of a control, just as the thoughtless drones that inhabit a beehive or anthill are controlled by the whims of their mistress.

Douglas (now Boeing) AGM-84 Harpoon/SLAM, and the Boeing AGM-86 Air Launched Cruise Missile (ALCM).

Target Drones

These aircraft evolved during World War II, as guidance technology reached the level of sophistication wherein large aircraft could be flown by remote control. Target drones were intended to be used to train fighter pilots or surface-to-air missile operators by giving them a full-size target to shoot at. Because such an aircraft could both take off and land by remote control, it occurred to their operators that they could be retrofitted with surveillance gear and used as reconnaissance platforms. These evolved into the first-generation UAVs.

Remotely Piloted Vehicles and Unmanned Aerial Vehicles

These are aircraft that are specifically designed to fly an entire mission profile just as an operational airplane would. They take off, fly somewhere to perform a specific task, return to their base, and land. They operate just like any other military aircraft would, except that there is no flesh-and-blood human aboard.

These aircraft were known as remotely piloted vehicles (RPVs) until the 1980s, but since that time, the term *unmanned aerial vehicles* (UAVs) has come into use as the preferred term. The latter is preferred because many of the modern drones are no longer remotely piloted—they are preprogrammed to operate *autonomously*. Operational examples of RPV/UAVs are the subject of this book.

Northrop Grumman developed this sleek, combat-capable concept for the U.S. Defense Advanced Research Projects Agency's (DARPA) quiet supersonic platform program. *Northrop Grumman Media Relations*

UNMANNED OR UNINHABITED?

The *U* in the acronym UAV stands for *unmanned*. There has been surprisingly little controversy over this gender-specific term, but there has been some. During the Clinton administration there was a brief flirtation with political correctness in which alternatives were explored. The term *unpiloted* was not applicable, because most of the UAVs flying today have pilots in remote locations; they just don't have a man or a woman aboard. Briefly, the nomenclature was rewritten as Uninhabited Aerial Vehicle. However, it must have been pointed out that no aircraft are ever actually *inhabited*. It has also been accepted that the term *man* is used as a generic term for humans as well as a specific term for male people. UAVs are now once again known as unmanned aerial vehicles. Of course it should be pointed out that a growing number of combat pilots in the American armed forces—including ground-bound UAV pilots—are women.

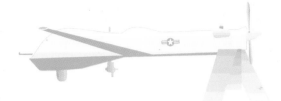

The Early Days of Unmanned Military Aircraft

The idea and technology of unmanned aircraft began with vehicles such as the Kettering Bug of World War I, and evolved through the first-generation cruise missiles during World War II and the decade following. Among the earliest were the small, flimsy, piston-engine, pilotless airplanes developed during World War I. In the United Kingdom, Harry Folland built one, while Professor A. M. Low experimented with television guidance and produced a radio-controlled rocket. In the United States, Dr. D. F. Buck built a piston-engine biplane designated *AT* for aerial torpedo, while Charles Kettering of the Delco Company built a similar vehicle that he called the Bug. The Bug was a precursor to modern RPVs and UAVs in that it was recoverable. With a range of over 60 miles, it was also quite advanced for its era. The U.S. Army Air Service ordered and tested large numbers of Kettering Bugs in 1918 and planned to send them into combat as cruise missiles—but the project was shelved when the war ended.

In the 1920s, Britain's Royal Aircraft Establishment built and tested the oddly named Larynx, a monoplane

LEFT: Crews are shown putting the final touches on Boeing's Project Compass Cope aircraft. The YQM-94A Gull would make its debut flight in July 1973. *U.S. Air Force*

The dapper Leigh Dugmore "Reginald" Denny was the unlikely father of the aircraft that were once known as remotely piloted vehicles (RPV), and which are now called unmanned aerial vehicles (UAVs). He was a Hollywood B-movie actor who pursued an interest in radio-controlled model airplanes in his spare time—or was it the other way around? *Author collection*

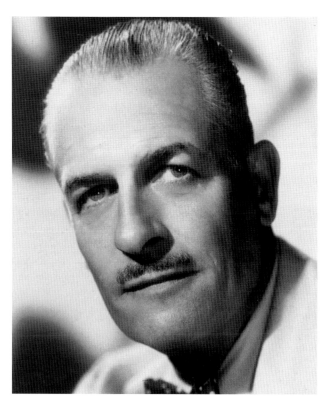

By the 1940s, Reg Denny had formed his Radioplane Company, and was spending more of his time at the factory, where he made drones for the U.S. Army Air Forces, than on the back lot at Paramount Studios, where they filmed his famous *Bulldog Drummond* pictures. *Author collection*

with a 100-mile range that was powered by a Lynx engine. Ironically, much of the testing of this remotely controlled airplane took place in the deserts of Iraq.

The Bugs and Larynxes were isolated projects that had no successors. The idea was there, but the roots of the RPV/UAV family tree were still a decade away from being planted. Though it was impossible to foresee it at the time, the line of evolution that led directly to modern UAVs had its origins in the 1930s. During that era, the aviation world was characterized by a great deal of tinkering by private individuals with limited budgets and unlimited imaginations. Numerous small companies came and went, while others survived to become industry-dominating giants. In tracing the UAV's evolutionary thread back to its start, one finds an origin so unconventional that it would be too improbable for a Hollywood movie. In fact, it begins in Hollywood—and with a Hollywood film star!

The unlikely father of the first generation of military UAVs was a B-movie actor named Leigh Dugmore Denny. Born in Britain in 1891, he immigrated to the United States after World War I and made his first Hollywood picture by 1919. Handsome and virile, he appeared in nearly two dozen short silent films during the 1920s under the name Reginald Denny. With the advent of the "talkies," he earned

First delivered to the U.S. Army Air Corps in November 1939, the Radioplane Model RP-4 was designated as OQ-1. It would be the first of a family of drones for which Radioplane would earn fleeting fame. Until the interest in UAVs later in the twentieth century sparked a resurgence of interest, the Radioplane drones were merely a forgotten footnote to World War II. *Author collection*

numerous roles as the stereotypical aloof Englishman in drawing-room comedies, and stardom as Algernon Longworth in Paramount's long series of *Bulldog Drummond* films in the late 1930s.

During the hours that he was not on the back lot, Reginald Denny indulged his passion of radio-controlled model airplanes. He even went so far as to open a hobby shop on Hollywood Boulevard. In 1934, he founded Denny Industries to manufacture radio-controlled (RC) model planes. As with many makers of full-size airplanes, this maker of models imagined that there was a military application for his radio-controlled planes, so, a year later, Denny formed the Radioplane Company to build larger RC aircraft. The RP-1, with wings spanning a dozen feet, was demonstrated to the U.S. Army, but there was no interest.

In 1938, Denny began working with Walter Righter, a fellow tinkerer and a graduate of Cal Tech in Pasadena, who was making miniature piston engines in his backyard shop in Burbank, about a half-hour's drive north of Hollywood. The result was a very sophisticated flying model called the Dennymite.

Early in 1938, the Army was ready to take a second look. It was not, however, the Air Corps. It was the Artillery Corps! Colonel C. M. Thiele at Fort MacArthur in San Pedro, about a half-hour south of Hollywood, asked for a demonstration. He saw the value of RC models for use as target practice for antiaircraft gunners. In May 1938, Reg Denny and Walter Righter were summoned to the Air Corps research and development center at Wright Field, Ohio. They came away with a contract for three experimental RC aircraft of a type that could be used as aerial targets. In 1940, the Air Corps contracted with Denny to construct large numbers of RC aerial targets. He opened a factory in Van Nuys, near Burbank, to manufacture them and brought Righter in as the chief engineer on the project. Righter soon returned to his own company, but this firm, the Righter Manufacturing Company, was acquired by Radioplane in 1945.

In the beginning, the Air Corps had planned to use the letter *A* to designate the RC aerial target aircraft, but this was obviously confusing because attack aircraft were also designated with this letter. By the beginning of 1942, the U.S. Army Air Forces discovered this, and the letter Q was added to its system of nomenclature to identify all unmanned aircraft—or "drones"—that were radio controlled or remote controlled. Initially, the Army would

The Lockheed Model 40 was one of a number of drones that were contemporaries of the Radioplanes, but were much less significant in terms of numbers. Only five Model 40s were built. *Author collection*

A Ryan Model 147J Lightning Bug low-altitude day photographic aircraft is seen here at Bien Hoa Air Base in April 1966. It is suspended from the number three pylon of a 99th Strategic Reconnaissance Squadron DC-130A and is ready for action. *Al Lloyd collection*

Photographed a split second after launch, this AQM-34L (Ryan Model 147SC) was equipped with a television camera in the nose that allowed the drone director aboard the DC-130 to guide it directly over the target. A general target area image was first displayed on the video monitor aboard the DC-130. *Al Lloyd collection*

This family picture of Ryan Firebee drones shows the types that flew for the 99th Strategic Reconnaissance Squadron. They include a Model 147J configured for low-altitude day photography (left); an extended-range Model 147H used for high-altitude missions (rear); a Model 147G, which was essentially a basic Model 147B with a larger engine (right); and a Model 147NX, used as a decoy or medium-altitude day photo reconnaissance drone. These are seen "in-country" at Bien Hoa Air Base near Saigon. *Al Lloyd collection*

This view of the 1940s-vintage launch system for the Lockheed Model 40 shows a contraption amazingly similar to that which would be used for UAVs such as the Sky Owl and the Pioneer a half century later. *Author collection*

designate its drones as *OQ*. This meant "radio-controlled model" rather than "observation drone," but this apparently random choice of letters was certainly auspicious in light of what would come to pass a half century later.

Other designations would be used through the years for various types of drones, but the letter *Q* would always be present in the nomenclature. It was used as a primary designation during the 1950s, but after 1962 it was relegated for use as a prefix to primary designation letters. In 1997, the Department of Defense would formally re-adopt *Q* as a primary designator.

World War II

After the United States entered World War II in December 1941, the quantity of purchase orders for all types of aircraft mushroomed. Reg Denny—and Radioplane—received thousands of orders for radio-controlled models. In fact, so many orders poured in after 1942 that Radioplane's Van Nuys plant could not handle them. The Frankfort Sailplane Company of Joliet, Illinois, would also build sizable numbers of the Radioplane designs under license.

The first Radioplane Model RP-4 aerial target officially ordered by the U.S. Army Air Forces was designated as OQ-1, and the initial production series of Model RP-5s were designated as OQ-2s. Each was powered by a 6.5-horsepower Righter engine. As various detail differences between production blocks were incorporated, new designations up through OQ-14 were introduced, although not all

went into large-scale production. Radioplane built about 50 OQ-1s, 600 OQ-2s, 5,822 OQ-3s, and 2,084 OQ-14s. Frankfort built 5,429 of these three types. Parenthetically, a sizable number of OQ aircraft were transferred to the U.S. Navy under the designation *TD* for target drone.

These first-generation Radioplane UAVs varied in length from 8 feet 8 inches to 9 feet 3 inches. The wingspans ranged from 12 feet 3 inches in the OQ-2 to 11 feet 6 inches in the OQ-14. The speed increased from 85 miles per hour to 140 miles per hour as the models incorporated larger and larger powerplants. The OQ-14 had a 22-horsepower engine. Each type had a duration in the air of about an hour.

World War II also saw numerous battlefield experiments with arming winged vehicles without pilots aboard. Germany produced and deployed the world's first operational cruise missile, the Fieseler Fi.103. This unmanned aircraft would be better known as the V-1, with the letter standing for *Vergeltungswaffe*, or Vengeance Weapon. The jet-propelled V-1s wreaked havoc on southern England during the summer of 1944, but they were simply terror weapons. They couldn't be used against specific targets because they lacked precision guidance.

The U.S. Army Air Forces also experimented with wartime cruise missiles. These included the Republic JB-2/KVW-1 Loon, which was based on the V-1, and the Northrop JB-10 Bat, an original concept. Neither became operational. As it was for the Germans, precision guidance was a problem

The AQM-34M Firebee, or Lightning Bug, was used in Southeast Asia in the Compass Bin and Buffalo Hunter operations. This one, nicknamed *Seagram*, is seen being hoisted from the tarpaulin to a dolly as part of the recovery process. Each drone was used for numerous missions. *Al Lloyd collection*

These two Hercules drone directors assigned to the 4080th Strategic Reconnaissance Wing can be identified as DC-130A aircraft by their three-bladed propellers. A Ryan Firebee drone can be seen suspended from the number two pylon of the nearest DC-130A. *Al Lloyd collection*

for the Americans. Indeed, resolving this dilemma would delay the deployment of truly reliable cruise missiles for more than three decades. However, once this problem was solved, it opened up a new world of possibilities upon which the UAVs of the twenty-first century are drawing.

For the U.S. Army Air Forces, the letter Q for drone was combined with the B for bomber nomenclature and applied to a series of secret "guided bomb" aircraft during World War II. Most were small, single-engine aircraft, but the BQ-7 Aphrodites were about two dozen converted B-17 Flying Fortresses, and the BQ-8 Anvils were several modified B-24 and PB4Y-1 Liberators. Both Anvil and Aphrodite were manned by a crew who flew the ship partway to the target. They then bailed out, turning control over to a remote pilot in another aircraft.

Packed with 25,000 pounds of Torpex high explosives, the BQ-8s had the largest nonnuclear payload of any missile in history. The first BQ-8 mission was flown in August 1944 against a German V-3 supergun weapon site near Calais, France, by Lieutenant Joseph Patrick Kennedy, the son of the former U.S. ambassador to the United Kingdom and the older brother of John F. Kennedy, the future president. Apparently, when Kennedy set the fuses in preparation for abandoning the BQ-8, they misfired and the Torpex exploded in midair. This was the first violent death in a series of such that would

plague the Kennedy family for over half a century. Three weeks later, a BQ-8 mission successfully obliterated a German base in Heligoland, Germany.

Postwar American RPVs

After the war, the U.S. Army Air Forces were divorced from the U.S. Army as the independent U.S. Air Force in 1947, and the nomenclature of remotely piloted vehicles parted into two separate lineages. The first generation of U.S. Air Force cruise missiles were designated with a B in the same series as manned bombers. These later were redesignated with a TM (tactical missile) or SM (strategic missile) prefix, but kept their number. The first generation of U.S. Air Force cruise missiles included the Martin B-61 (later TM-61) Matador, the Northrop B-62 (later SM-62) Snark, the North American B-64 (later SM-64) Navajo, and the Martin B-76 (later TM-76) Mace.

Meanwhile, the Q nomenclature reverted to aircraft that were strictly remotely controlled drones, which were used mainly as aerial targets. The letter was assigned as a prefix to conversions from previously manned aircraft. For example, a sizable number of now-obsolete B-17s became QB-17s. Most of these were destroyed in postwar surface-to-air missile tests.

The letter also went to a new series of aircraft purposely built as remotely powered aircraft under

A DC-130 lifts off on a muggy Southeast Asia morning for a mission in the north with a pair of AQM-34M drones suspended from its number two and three pylons. *Al Lloyd collection*

A DC-130 of the 4080th Strategic Reconnaissance Wing DC-130 heads north out of Bien Hoa Air Base on an operational mission. Suspended from the number two and three pylons are a Ryan Model 147G and a longer-winged Model 147H. *Al Lloyd collection*

the auspices of the Air Force's new Pilotless Aircraft Branch. In Van Nuys, Radioplane received the first contract for a new "Q-plane." The Q-1 was a pulsejet-powered target drone designed to be air launched by a Douglas B-26. It had landing gear that allowed it to land after a mission for re-use. Only 28 experimental XQ-1s were built before the program was terminated, but the engineering work later evolved into the GAM-77 Crossbow air-launched antiradar missile. The XQ-1A was 20 feet long, and the XQ-1B was 18 feet 4 inches long. Both had straight wings spanning 14 feet 5 inches. As with Radioplane's wartime aircraft, their duration aloft was about an hour.

In 1952, Radioplane was acquired by the Northrop Corporation as its Radioplane Division. Northrop would later rename the unit the Ventura Division. Meanwhile, Radioplane's founder, Reginald Denny, would continue to live in southern California until June 1967, when he died at the age of 75.

In 1953, the Radioplane Division began work on the Q-4, a jet-propelled RPV that was intended to be

Taken on October 6, 1968, by a fast-moving Ryan Model 147S low-altitude photo reconnaissance drone, this picture shows a group of seven operational antiaircraft artillery batteries that have been disguised to look like SA-2 Guideline missile sites. The inset image is from the vehicle's 180-degree panoramic camera. *Al Lloyd collection*

This AQM-34M Buffalo Hunter has just been recovered by a Sikorsky CH-3 Jolly Green Giant. The helicopter is depositing the drone on a huge tarpaulin in preparation for its being loaded onto a dolly for transport. *Al Lloyd collection*

capable of supersonic speeds. The XQ-4A was 33 feet long, with a wingspan of 11 feet 1 inch. First flown in 1961, the Q-4B was about 28 inches longer, with a wingspan of 12 feet 8 inches. A total of 25 examples of the two types were built, but the program was terminated before these became operational.

Meanwhile, the Q-2 designation went to the aircraft that would evolve into the most successful jet-propelled American drone of the twentieth century—the Ryan Firebee. More than 6,500 would be built over the ensuing half century by the Ryan Aeronautical Company, founded by T. Claude Ryan. The company was later acquired by Northrop Grumman.

Born in Kansas in 1898, Claude Ryan learned to fly in the U.S. Army Air Service during World War I. He relocated to San Diego in 1922, where he started the first of many companies that would bear his name. He operated airlines and flight schools, and he built airplanes. Among the most famous of these was the Ryan NYP, better known as Charles Lindbergh's *Spirit of St. Louis*.

During World War II, Ryan built more than a thousand primary trainers under the PT-20 and PT-22 designations, all of which were based on his prewar Model ST sport plane. Late in the war, as jet propulsion technology began to evolve, Ryan built the U.S. Navy's first hybrid fighter aircraft,

In this extremely rare image, we see an AQM-34M riding on a 99th Strategic Reconnaissance Squadron DC-130 that is flying in formation with a manned U-2R reconnaissance aircraft over Southeast Asia. Maximum results were achieved by teaming U-2Rs with Firebees that were equipped with LORAN (long-range radio aid for navigation). *Al Lloyd collection*

combining piston-engine power with an auxiliary jet engine. Only 69 of these FR-1 Fireballs were built, but the exercise got Ryan started with jet aircraft.

In 1948, Ryan received the Air Force contract for the Q-2, a jet-propelled target drone for both surface-to-air and air-to-air gunnery training. The first flight of the XQ-2 came early in 1951, and the Firebee entered production as the Q-2A for the Air Force and as the KDA-01 for the U.S. Navy. It was 17 feet 3 inches long, with swept wings spanning 11 feet 2 inches. Powered by either a Continental J69 or a Fairchild J44 turbojet engine, it had a top speed of Mach .9 and a range of 400 miles. Its duration was just under an hour, and it was capable of operating above 50,000 feet.

Operationally, Firebees could be air launched, or surface launched with an Aerojet General X102 solid-fuel rocket booster engine. Unlike the wartime remote-controlled OQ aircraft, it was not recovered through the use of landing gear on a runway, but rather with a remotely deployed parachute system.

The larger Q-2C Firebee (Ryan Model 124) made its first flight in December 1958. It was 22 feet 11 inches long, with a wingspan of 12 feet 11 inches. Powered by an improved Continental J69, it had a range of 800 miles—double that of the Q-2A—and could operate above 60,000 feet. Like the Q-2A, its speed was just short of supersonic. The Q-2C Firebee's signature feature was probably its distinctive engine intake, which looked like a laughing mouth beneath the long, sharply pointed, sharklike nose.

In 1962, two years after the Q-2C entered production, the Defense Department reorganized its nomenclature system. At that time, the Q for drone prefix was merged with the M for missile, and drones were renumbered in the missile lineage. (The Q designation would be reinstituted in 1997, with the Predator as the new Q-1.)

Under the new nomenclature, the Air Force's Q-2C became the BQM-34A, while the U.S. Navy's KDA-1 and KDA-2 Firebees became BQM-34B and BQM-34C. Those Firebees used by the U.S. Army would be designated as MQM-34D. As used here, the B prefix implied that a particular drone operated from multiple launch platforms, not that it was a bomber. The Firebee would remain in production under the new designation until 1982, 13 years after Ryan Aeronautical was acquired by Teledyne and renamed Teledyne Ryan. (In turn, in 1999 Teledyne Ryan would become part of the Northrop Grumman Corporation.) In 1986, under the Reagan administration, production was restarted, with additional aircraft being produced as BGM-34S.

Meanwhile, in the mid-1960s, the natural next step in Firebee evolution had been the supersonic Ryan Model 166, which was ordered by the U.S. Navy in 1965 under the designation BQM-34E. Known officially as the Firebee II, it made its first flight in January 1968 and became operational in 1972. The U.S. Air Force ordered the Firebee II in 1969 under the designation BQM-34F. It was similar to the BQM-34E, but it was designed to be retrieved in midair by a helicopter as it was descending by parachute. This scenario was first tested in 1971.

The Firebee II aircraft were 29 feet 2 inches long, with a wingspan of 8 feet 11 inches. They were powered by a Continental J69-T-406 turbojet and had a top speed of Mach 1.1. The range was nearly 900 miles, with a ceiling of 60,000 feet. The endurance was more than an hour. The range could be extended through the use of a conformal external tank, but this limited the speed to less than Mach 1. There would be 50 Firebee IIs built before production ended in 1980.

While the Firebee originated as a target drone and long continued to be used as such, it was also one of the first recoverable RPVs to be widely used in a reconnaissance role. It was during the 1960s that the U.S. Air Force took a first step toward the widespread use of adapting their RPVs for use as something other than just target drones.

BQM-34 Firebees that continued in service after the war in Southeast Asia were typically repainted in high-visibility orange, whereas during the war, they were usually painted in light gray for daytime operations, or black for night. The small number that were used in Gulf War II in 2003 wore dark gray war paint. *Northrop Grumman Media Relations*

A Chukar III is launched from the deck of an unidentified vessel belonging to the navy of one of Northrop's many export customers for the product. Note the Phalanx gun and the six missile tubes aft of the helicopter pad. The absence of U.S. national insignia identifies this vehicle as an export model Chukar III. Essentially identical to the U.S. Navy BQM-74E, the international Chukar III was widely deployed among NATO countries in the 1980s. *Northrop Grumman Media Relations*

Firebees and Lightning Bugs at War

In 1961, the U.S. Air Force ordered a reconnaissance variation of the Firebee under the project code-named *Fire Fly*. Ryan had retrofitted a BQM-34A with new navigation and surveillance equipment and additional fuel capacity, and this aircraft was first flight-tested between April and August 1962 under the nonmilitary designation Model 147A. Two years later, a family of Model 147s went to war.

Known as Lightning Bugs, the Model 147s used in Southeast Asia were controlled by both the U.S. Air Force and the Central Intelligence Agency (CIA). The latter was responsible for the design and management of specific equipment packages. The U.S. Navy, meanwhile, operated the Model 147SK. Launched with a rocket booster from the aircraft carrier USS *Ranger* in the South China Sea, the Navy Bugs were operational between November 1969 and June 1970.

The vast majority of Lightning Bug operations for the first three years of the Southeast Asia deployment were high-altitude photo-reconnaissance missions. These were conducted between August 1964 and the end of 1965 by Model 147Bs, which

had been specially modified with an enlarged wing. These aircraft were succeeded by the longer Model 147G, which remained in action until August 1967. Between them, these two types conducted 161 missions. During this time, Models 147D and 147E were used for a small number of electronic intelligence missions in 1965 and 1966.

The Bugs were air launched from DC-130A and DC-130E "mother ships," or drone director aircraft, of which at least 15 were converted from Lockheed C-130 Hercules transports. The Lightning Bugs were recovered by parachute. In some cases after 1969, these descending Bugs were snatched in midair by helicopters outfitted with the mid-air retrieval system (MARS).

Air Force Bugs were assigned to the 100th Strategic Reconnaissance Wing of the Air Force Strategic Air Command. In the autumn of 1968, the Air Force began using the AQM-34 designation, rather than BQM-34, to classify its reconnaissance Lightning Bugs operating in Southeast Asia. The first Air Force Lightning Bugs operating in the theater to be assigned the *AQM* prefix were the AQM-34Gs, which were manufactured and deployed under the Air Force Compass Bin and Buffalo Hunter programs that

A Northrop BQM-74E is shown mounted on the number three pylon of a U.S. Navy DC-130 drone carrier. This pylon is obviously adaptable for payloads larger than the Chukar. *Northrop Grumman Media Relations*

This photograph depicts a rocket-assisted takeoff of a Northrop BQM-74E Chukar. The basic weight of the drone is 465 pounds. The booster, used in surface launches but not air launches, adds 130 pounds. *Northrop Grumman Media Relations*

succeeded the earlier Combat Angel program. The AQM-34Gs were configured to aid manned strike aircraft by conducting electronic countermeasures and laying radar-confusing chaff ahead of them as they entered enemy airspace. The nighttime reconnaissance Bug, designated as AQM-34K, flew 44 missions between November 1968 and October 1969.

The majority of Lightning Bug operations were low-altitude, mainly photo-reconnaissance missions. These Lightning Bugs got down and dirty at as low as 500 feet, where the antiaircraft gunners did not see them until they were practically gone. Manufactured and deployed under the Air Force Compass Bin and Buffalo Hunter programs, the AQM-34L flew 1,773 low-altitude missions between January 1969 and June 1973. Most of these were photo-reconnaissance flights, but 121 missions, flown after June 1972, involved real-time television imaging. This made the AQM-34L RPV a true precursor of twenty-first-century UAVs.

With the mist-shrouded hills east of Point Mugu, California, forming a moody backdrop, this DC-130 drone carrier taxis toward the runway with a brace of four Northrop BQM-74E Chukars. *Northrop Grumman Media Relations*

Another mission that demonstrated a RPV/UAV capability that would be revived in the twenty-first century was in the area of signals intelligence. In the mid-1960s, Airborne Command and Control Centers (ABCCC, the predecessor of today's Airborne Warning and Control System [AWACS]) were located aboard Lockheed EC-121 Constellations, operating in conjunction with other electronic warfare assets under such operational code names as *College Eye* and *Big Eye*. Their job, like today's AWACS, was to patrol the Gulf of Tonkin, monitoring North Vietnamese radio frequencies. It was dangerous work for an unarmed, manned aircraft operating so close to enemy territory. When an EC-121 was lost, the Air Force decided to use a drone for this mission. The Combat Dawn project led to production of specially configured AQM-34Q electronic surveillance aircraft. These were operational on 268 missions from February 1970 to June 1973, providing real-time electronic intelligence.

After the Paris Peace Accords of 1973 ended major U.S. military involvement in Vietnam, the reconnaissance mission continued. Until April 1975, when North Vietnam successfully conquered South Vietnam, 183 low-level real-time imaging missions were flown by AQM-34M Lightning Bugs (Model 147H). The AQM-34Ms had earlier been used to fly 138 high-altitude photo-reconnaissance missions between March 1967 and July 1971. The AQM-34Ms occasionally operated at altitudes as low as 200 feet. Meanwhile, as the AQM-34Q Combat Dawn signals intelligence aircraft were phased out, they were superseded by the longer-range AQM-34R aircraft, which flew 216 missions between February 1973 and June 1975 with a 97 percent success rate.

Between 1964 and 1975, the Lightning Bug fleet flew 3,435 operational missions in the Southeast Asia Theater. More than half of these were by AQM-34Ls. Without the peril of losing a pilot, the

The Boeing YQM-94A Gull is in flight high above the clouds. The design objective of the Compass Cope program was a service ceiling of 70,000 feet. In this sense, and in terms of endurance objectives, Compass Cope's Gull and Tern were the 1970s precursors to that turn-of-the-century bird called Global Hawk. *U.S. Air Force*

A Gull at sunrise: the first Boeing YQM-94A awaits its first flight on the hard surface of the dry lake as the sun rises on the Compass Cope program, the first effort by the U.S. Air Force to develop a high-flying, long-endurance reconnaissance drone. *U.S. Air Force*

Lightning Bugs could fly into the most dangerous of places, and they did. In short, the Air Force had discovered that RPVs were good for missions that were "dull, dirty, and dangerous."

The individual Bugs lasted an average of 7.3 missions before they were lost, but one AQM-34L, nicknamed *Tomcat*, successfully returned from 67 missions before being lost on its 68th. Certain missions had higher success rates. As may have been expected, more than half of the Lightning Bugs used as decoys and for especially dangerous night missions were lost. On the early high-altitude missions only 6 in 10 returned. However, the later low-level reconnaissance missions counted on a better than 90 percent success rate.

In addition to using drones as reconnaissance aircraft, the U.S. Air Force also experimented with using them as precursors to twenty-first-century UCAVs. Early in 1971, under the Have Lemon project, Firebees were experimentally armed with various types of ordnance, including Hughes AGM-65 Maverick ground-attack missiles and Rockwell GBU-8 Stubby Hobo glide bomb units.

The first live-fire test of a guided air-to-surface missile launched from an American RPV came on December 14, 1971. A Firebee being tested by the 6514th Test Squadron at the Edwards Air Force Base Flight Test Center scored a direct hit with a Maverick on an obsolete radar van parked on the test range. A second Maverick test one week later was also successful, as were two Stubby Hobo tests in February 1972.

Both the Maverick and the Stubby Hobo—like the Firebee itself—were electro-optically guided, meaning that the controller at a remote-control van could watch the UAV's progress on television as though he was aboard. When the weapon was launched, he could then switch screens from the drone to the weapon and guide it to the target.

Though the Have Lemon UCAVs were theoretically ready for action by the time of the Operation Linebacker I offensive in May 1972, they were never deployed. The most dangerous and highest-value targets assigned to the Have Lemon drones would have been enemy air defenses, and with 1972 imaging technology, these would have been hard to see and hit if they were well camouflaged.

After the end of the war in Southeast Asia, the U.S. Air Force terminated the use of Firebees and Lightning Bugs in the reconnaissance role. However, the success that the Air Force had experienced with those vehicles during the war led to experimentation with other missions. The Air Force revisited the old Combat Angel project by contracting with Ryan to retrofit approximately five dozen existing surplus Lightning Bugs with electronic radar jammers and such equipment as AN/ALE-38 chaff dispensers. Redelivered under the designation AQM-34V, these aircraft were supplemented by an additional 16 factory-fresh aircraft. The AQM-34Vs were tested between 1976 and 1978, but were then withdrawn from service.

Of the other Lightning Bugs remaining after the Vietnam War, some became museum pieces, many went into long-term storage, some continued to serve as aerial targets for missile development tests, and about 33 were transferred to the Israeli Air Force. During the Yom Kippur War of 1973, the Israelis successfully deployed their drones as decoys to divert antiaircraft fire from manned bombers. The

Israelis have used UAVs in the reconnaissance role continuously since the 1970s.

A fitting postscript to the career of the Firebee was the use of the little drones during the opening phase of Gulf War II in March 2003. These vehicles were used on the first night of the war to lay chaff corridors through Iraqi airspace to shield cruise missiles and manned aircraft on strike missions to Baghdad and other targets deep inside Iraq. With the Firebee's twenty-first-century mission accomplished, there was even some discussion of restarting the production line!

MQM-74/BQM-74 Chukar

If we begin our study of American military RPV/UAVs with the Radioplane drones of Reginald Denny and trace that lineage forward in time, the last major operational drone in the line is the MQM-74/BQM-74 Chukar. Named for a ground-dwelling game bird indigenous to the Midwestern United States, the Chukar was created by the Ventura Division of the Northrop Corporation, which is what Radioplane became after Northrop acquired the company. Ironically, it had many features in common with the Ryan Firebee, which became a Northrop product in 1999 when Northrop Grumman acquired Ryan Aeronautical.

First delivered to the U.S. Navy in 1968—the year after Reg Denny passed away—the jet-propelled Chukar evolved from the Northrop Ventura Model NV-105 as a proposal for a U.S. Navy requirement for an aerial target for antiaircraft gunnery and missile training. The original delta-winged design of 1964 was superseded by a straight-winged NV-105A a year later. This vehicle was ordered for production by the Navy under the designation MQM-74A. Powered by a Williams J400-WR-400 turbojet engine, the MQM-74A was designed to be launched from a ship using a rocket-assist system. The MQM-74A was 11 feet 4 inches long, with a wingspan of 5 feet 7 inches, and it weighed 425 pounds. An improved MQM-74B was evaluated, but it was not produced in large numbers.

For the Chukar, in-flight tracking was passive. The operator had to either be able to see the Chukar's flight path or track it on radar. If a particular vehicle was to be recovered, rather than expended on a mission, the operator could deploy a parachute. Contrary to the Chukar's ground-dwelling namesake, the MQM-74A and all subsequent Chukars were capable of operating at altitudes as high as 40,000 feet.

This is a top view of Boeing's YQM-94A Gull UAV as it is towed from the factory. Powered by a General Electric TF34 turbofan, the YQM-94A demonstrated an endurance of more than 17 hours. *U.S. Air Force*

Beginning in 1974, the U.S. Navy started taking delivery of the MQM-74C Chukar II, which was 12 feet 8 inches long, with a wingspan of 5 feet 9 inches. It weighed in at just under 500 pounds and had a range of nearly 400 miles, half again more than the MQM-74A. Powered by a J400-WR-401 turbojet, it had a top speed of 575 miles per hour, again a marked improvement over its predecessor.

In the late 1970s, both the U.S. Army and the U.S. Air Force studied the Chukar II for possible adaptation as top-secret reconnaissance vehicles. The Army version was to have been designated as BQM-74D, but a production model was apparently not produced. The Air Force version was evaluated under the Tactical Expendable Drone System (TEDS). As with the Army's BQM-74D, this secret project is believed to have been terminated.

In the meantime, Northrop proceeded with the BQM-74C for the U.S. Navy, of which a sizable number were produced during the 1980s. The BQM-74C was also known as the Chukar III, the name used by Northrop as the principal designation of the export version of this drone. First deployed by North Atlantic Treaty Organization (NATO) countries in Europe in 1984, the Chukar III was still in service at the turn of the century in France, Spain, and the United Kingdom, as well as Japan, Taiwan, and Singapore. The company produced more than 1,150 Chukars for its international customers.

The BQM-74C Chukar III was 12 feet 11 inches long, with a wingspan identical to that of its predecessor. This variant incorporated an optional onboard video system for reconnaissance missions and was designed to be air launched as well as sur-

A Northrop BQM-74E Chukar flies over the Pacific during flight trials. The 540-knot vehicle joined the fleet in 1992.

face launched. The lighter, air-launched version had a range of more than 500 miles; like the Firebees, they were launched from Lockheed DC-130 mother ships. During Gulf War I, BQM-74Cs, as well as Firebees, were used with reported success as decoy aircraft, drawing Iraqi antiaircraft fire away from manned strike aircraft.

Beginning in 1992, the U.S. Navy began taking delivery of the BQM-74E Chukar. The same size as the BQM-74C, the new drone has a top speed of 620 miles per hour and a range of nearly 750 miles.

An estimated 3,200 MQM-74A and MQM-74C drones were produced, and through the turn of the century, about 2,000 BQM-74C and BQM-74E vehicles were delivered. In 2003, after the BQM-74s were used—along with Firebees—as chaff dispensers during Gulf War II, plans for a further, improved BQM-74F were accelerated.

Tagboard and Senior Bowl

Just as the Lockheed SR-71 Blackbird was the fastest manned reconnaissance aircraft known to have flown during the twentieth century, the related D-21 reconnaissance UAV is the fastest of its kind known to have flown during the past century. Unlike the subsonic Lightning Bugs of the Vietnam era, or the lumbering UAVs of today, the D-21 was capable of flying at three times the speed of sound.

Like the SR-71, the D-21 was created in the wake of the highly publicized shootdown over the Soviet Union of a U-2 spy plane on May Day in 1960. This incident emphasized the need for a spy plane that could fly faster than Soviet surface-to-air missiles. At Lockheed, Kelly Johnson's Advanced Research Projects department, known as the Skunk Works, would meet this demand.

The idea for the D-21 program originated with Johnson, who saw it as a natural extension of the SR-71 (originally designated as A-12) program. He could see the value of a Mach-3 reconnaissance drone that could be air launched by the Mach-3 A-12/SR-71 aircraft. No aircraft in the world was fast enough to catch either one, so they could operate with impunity in any hostile airspace.

This dramatic view shows a Lockheed D-21 Tagboard drone under construction at Burbank. It is rotated 90 degrees in the jig so that crews can work on the starboard wing. *Lockheed*

31

The CIA, Lockheed's original customer for the A-12, showed little initial interest in the Mach-3 UAV, but in October 1962 they finally authorized the project under the code name *Tagboard*. As with the A-12/SR-71 program, the Tagboard drone originated as a CIA project, but in both programs, the U.S. Air Force would ultimately emerge as the dominant player.

Lockheed referred to their new drone aircraft as the Q-12, implying that it was to be a drone associated with the A-12. In 1963, as the two aircraft evolved as a joint weapons system, the A-12 carrier aircraft were redesignated with an *M* for mother ship, and the Q-12 was designated with a *D* for drone, or daughter ship. To avoid confusion with other A-12s that would not be used with Tagboard, the numerals were also inverted. Thus, it would be a D-21 drone aboard an M-21 mother ship.

This rare view shows a Compass Cope control station that is, at first glance, much like those used for twenty-first-century UAVs such as a Predator or Global Hawk. However, this 1974-vintage cathode ray tube (CRT) screen is a far cry from modern liquid crystal color. *U.S. Air Force*

In developing the D-21, Lockheed drew upon past experience with their X-7 experimental aircraft and their working relationship with the Marquardt Company, whose RJ43 ramjet engines would be used. The operational D-21 would be 42 feet 10 inches long, with a wingspan of 19 feet. Like the A-12/M-21/SR-71, it would have a top speed in excess of Mach 3 and a service ceiling above 100,000 feet. Its range, once launched from the mother ship, would exceed 3,000 miles. The D-21 was designed to be recovered by parachute after it ejected a module containing sensor gear, its reconnaissance camera, and film exposed on its mission.

Wind-tunnel and other tests took place during 1963, and the first D-21 was completed in August 1964. The debut flight of a D-21 mated to the rear top fuselage of its mother ship occurred at Groom Lake (Area 51) in Nevada in December 1964, and the first air launch and free flight of a D-21 followed in March 1966.

After three successful launches, a D-21 malfunction on the fourth flight resulted in the loss of both drone and mother ship, as well as one of the mother-ship crew. In the wake of this incident, Kelly Johnson proposed that they switch to using a B-52H as a mother ship. This new launch scenario would be code-named *Senior Bowl*, and the drones themselves would be modified and redesignated as D-21B. In the Senior Bowl operations, the drones would be launched at subsonic speeds, but the D-21B could be carried *under* the mother ship; hence it could be *dropped* rather than *launched* from the top of another aircraft. After a series of failed launches, the first successful Senior Bowl launch of a D-21B from a B-52H occurred in June 1968.

After more testing, the CIA and the Air Force requested and received presidential authorization to use the D-21B on an operational photo-reconnaissance mission over North Vietnam. In November 1969, the first such deployment failed when the data link malfunctioned and the D-21B "vanished." Three further operational missions between December 1970 and March 1971 were all deemed as failures when the camera modules were lost or damaged in recovery.

The Tagboard/Senior Bowl/D-21 program was officially cancelled in July 1971, although its existence would remain classified as top secret until 1977.

Compass Cope

Even as the Lightning Bugs were flying mostly tactical missions in Southeast Asia, the U.S. Air Force was considering RPV/UAVs for much-longer-duration strategic missions. Just as the Tagboard project envisioned a UAV roughly analogous in performance to the Lockheed SR-71 spy plane, the Compass Cope program of 1971 envisioned a vehicle roughly analogous to the Lockheed U-2 spy plane. As with the U-2, Compass Cope was a slow aircraft with an emphasis on very long endurance (up to 24 hours) at very high altitudes (above 70,000 feet). Compass Cope control would be by way of a real-time television data link to a ground-based operator. In addition to reconnaissance, the platform could be tasked with communications relay and atmospheric sampling. Like the earlier Radioplane drones, the Compass Cope would be intended to take off and land on runways, rather than being air launched like D-21s or Firebees.

There would be two actual aircraft types built as flight-test vehicles under the Compass Cope program. The first would be the Boeing Model 901, ordered as the YQM-94A Gull (Compass Cope B), which was originally envisioned as the only Compass Cope type. Boeing had been considered as a single source for Compass Cope, but Teledyne Ryan proposed its Model 235 as a possible contender. Approved by the Department of Defense, this type would be ordered as the YQM-98A Tern (Compass Cope R). Both aircraft, like the U-2, had long wings like those of a sailplane, which made for extended range and endurance. This feature continues to be an important characteristic of twenty-first-century UAVs, such as the RQ-4 Global Hawk, which originated as a Teledyne Ryan program.

For Compass Cope, the Boeing Gull would be an all-new aircraft, but the Tern had its roots in the Teledyne Ryan Model 154, which had been built for an earlier Air Force project code-named *Compass Arrow*. The Model 154 aircraft was code-named *Firefly*, which implies a relationship with Operation Fire Fly, the version of the first Ryan Model 147A Firebee adapted for use as a reconnaissance aircraft in 1962. (The real relationship, if any, remains a secret, never officially confirmed.) Not unlike Compass Cope, the idea of the Compass Arrow project had been for a high-altitude photo-reconnaissance aircraft capable of a deep penetration into Chinese airspace. Such a mission was beyond the range of the Firebee or Chukar families and too dangerous for a manned U-2.

Compass Arrow was initiated in 1966, and the Model 154 made its debut flight in June 1968. Officially designated as AQM-91 in 1970, the Firefly was powered by one General Electric J97 turbojet engine. It was 34 feet 2 inches long, with a wingspan of 47 feet 8 inches. It had a service ceiling of 78,000 feet and a range of 4,370 miles. Like the Lightning Bug drones then active over Southeast Asia, it was air launched from a DC-130, and it was recovered with MARS. Nearly two dozen production-series AQM-91s were built, but they were reportedly scrapped without having been used operationally.

The Ryan YQM-98A Compass Cope R made its first flight in August 1974 and went on to set a world endurance record for an unmanned, unrefueled aircraft, of 28 hours, 11 minutes. The twin-tailed Tern was powered by a Garrett YF104 turbofan engine, which was mounted on its back to reduce its radar signature. It was 37 feet 4 inches long, with a wingspan of 81 feet 2 inches.

The first prototype Boeing YQM-94A Gull had made its debut flight in July 1973, but it crashed a few days later on its second flight. The flight-test program continued with the second YQM-94A, until November 1974. The Gull was 40 feet long with its nose probe, and it had a wingspan of 90 feet. It was powered by a General Electric TF34 turbofan, which was, like the engine in the Tern, mounted above the fuselage. During the flight-test program, the YQM-94A demonstrated an endurance of more than 17 hours.

In August 1976, the Boeing YQM-94A was chosen over the competition, and a production contract was issued for a series of YQM-94B aircraft. Having produced what it felt was a superior (albeit more expensive) aircraft, Teledyne Ryan lodged a protest. It was a moot point, as the Air Force cancelled the Compass Cope project in July 1977 before any further aircraft were built.

The respective plane makers would go on to bigger and better things in the UAV world—Boeing to the Condor and Ryan to the Global Hawk.

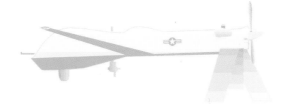

CHAPTER
TWO

Battlefield UAVs of the Late Cold War Era

fter the end of the Vietnam War, interest in UAVs waned considerably within the U.S. military. The D-21 was canceled, the Lightning Bugs were mothballed, and Compass Cope was stillborn. A few projects would be discussed during the last decades of the Cold War, and some research work done, but it would not be until the 1980s, and the eve of Gulf War I, that American forces in the field would have UAVs at their disposal.

Ironically, the Gulf War I generation of UAVs would be the offspring not of the American initiatives of the 1960s, but the Israeli initiatives of the 1980s that led to the Hunter UAV, which was developed by Israel Aircraft Industries (IAI) and which evolved into the widely used Pioneer. The UAV paradigm of the 1980s had more in common with Reginald Denny's RC models from the 1940s than it did with D-21s and Firebees. The emphasis was, once again, on simplicity and economy over extreme high performance. As represented by the Israeli-designed Hunter and its

cousins, this new paradigm is visible in a common design for the vast majority of the deployed UAVs during this era—straight wings, pusher propellers, and twin booms with twin tails. The pusher prop was used so that the drones could be recovered by nosing into a net, since a forward-mounted tractor prop would damage both the drone and the net.

During the 1973 Yom Kippur War, many Israeli battlefield commanders had observed the need for an "over-the-horizon" reconnaissance system, and this planted a seed that would, in time, grow into a new generation of UAVs. During the 1970s, Israeli defense contractors pursued the technology on their own initiative.

By the end of the decade, two small Israeli UAVs had emerged. First was the Mastiff, created by Tadiran Electronics, followed by the Scout, developed by IAI, the country's major plane maker. Both were roughly the same size as Reg Denny's early Radioplane drones, and like the Radioplane drones, they were powered by a single, simple gasoline engine. The relative wingspans were 13 feet 11 inches for the Mastiff and 16 feet 3 inches for the Scout. They both had straight wings and a tail mounted on twin booms, with a pusher prop between the booms on the rear of the fuselage. Surveillance equipment centered on a small video camera with a real-time

LEFT: Though the vehicle was equipped with a centerline landing skid, the preferable means of recovering the McDonnell Douglas Sky Owl was by parachute. This, and snagging by net, would be the standard recovery procedures for most tactical UAVs through the end of the Cold War. *McDonnell Douglas*

35

First flown in 1973, the Developmental Sciences R4E SkyEye was a remarkably advanced UAV for its day. During the 1980s, the U.S. Army flew them operationally in covert missions in Central America and possibly elsewhere. Seen here is a later model, the R4E-50, circa 1986. *Author collection*

data link to an operator on the ground. Like the Radioplane UAVs, they had landing gear to facilitate runway operations.

By the early 1980s, official indifference gave way to a strong interest by the Israeli military in UAVs. A stiff competition between IAI and Tadiran culminated in a truce and a decision by the two companies in early 1984 to form a joint UAV development company to be known as Mazlat.

In the meantime, the little Israeli UAVs had experienced their baptism of fire during the 1982 conflict in Lebanon and had proven themselves invaluable to battlefield commanders. Among other things, the UAVs successfully spotted—and facilitated the destruction of—more than two dozen Syrian surface-to-air missile sites hidden in the Bekaa Valley.

Typical of the twin-boom, pusher-prop UAVs of the late Cold War period was the McDonnell Douglas Sky Owl, which was based on the R4E SkyEye. It is seen here during a December 1991 flight-test. *McDonnell Douglas*

This 1991 forward view of the McDonnell Douglas Sky Owl provides a good look at the surveillance camera turret in the vehicle's chin. An operational turret might have accommodated both low-light television (LLTV) and forward-looking infrared (FLIR) imaging devices. *McDonnell Douglas*

The success of the small drones was not lost on battlefield commanders in the United States, who had been through their own recent battles in Lebanon and Grenada. There was interest in these UAVs on the part of both the U.S. Marine Corps and the U.S. Navy, but there was also a reluctance to buy aircraft from an offshore firm. This problem was solved by Mazlat working through the Maryland-based AAI Corporation. In 1985, AAI began working with the U.S. services to develop what was to evolve into the RQ-2 Pioneer UAV used by U.S. forces.

Meanwhile, Mazlat (Malat after 1988) continued to develop UAVs for the Israeli armed forces. The result was the Searcher UAV, which entered service in 1992. Essentially a scaled-up Scout, it has a wingspan of 25 feet 1 inch and is 16 feet 8 inches long. The

Searcher II, introduced in 1998, is 19 feet 2 inches long, with a wingspan of 28 feet.

Another, smaller, vehicle developed in the United States is the AeroVironment FQM-151 Pointer, which was used in Operations Desert Shield and Desert Storm as well as in the war on terror operations in the early twenty-first century. Initially delivered in 1989, the FQM-151A Pointer has served with the U.S. Army, U.S. Air Force, and the U.S. Marine Corps. As of the turn of the century, it has also been operated by France's Armee de Terre (land army).

Made of a Kevlar composite material, the Pointer is 6 feet long, with a wingspan of 8 feet 3 inches, and it has a takeoff weight of about 8 pounds. The system's ground-control unit weighs just over 17 pounds. It has a patrol radius of 5 miles

The McDonnell Douglas Sky Owl is placed on its launch rail in preparation for a flight-test in January 1992, six months after the first flight. *McDonnell Douglas*

from the controller, with a flight duration time of 90 minutes and a top speed of 50 miles per hour. The onboard camera system, using either color video or infrared night vision, can record imagery to an onboard recorder or relay live video images to a ground station. The battery-powered Pointer is a quiet and unobtrusive reconnaissance platform.

Described as a "back-packable, hand-launched" UAV, the Pointer is easy to use and requires minimal operator training because it incorporates stability augmentation avionics. This includes AutoNavigation and a soft-vertical-descent "AutoLand" capability. The FQM-151A was originally designed as a tactical reconnaissance, surveillance, and remote-monitoring vehicle with both military and law-enforcement applications, and sensor payloads permit the surveillance mission to be expanded to encompass detection of chemical or biological weapons.

A number of European and American UAVs of the 1980s shared the twin-boom, pusher-prop configuration of the contemporary Israeli Mastiff and Scout drones. British Aerospace Dynamics developed and tested the 180-pound Stabileye drone during 1984. Designed to be launched with a pneumatic launch system, Stabileye was intended to fly nocturnal tactical missions at altitudes up to 10,000 feet, returning real-time infrared images. From Italy, the Meteor Mirach 100 was adapted by Pacific Aerosystems of San Diego as its Heron 26. This UAV was evaluated by the U.S. Navy in the mid-1980s in an unsuccessful competition with the Pioneer.

The Model R4 series SkyEye was created by Developmental Sciences, a company that became the Astronautics Division of Lear Siegler in 1984. The SkyEye was first flown experimentally in 1973 by Developmental Sciences, and the improved R4D

This is how the McDonnell Douglas Sky Owl might have appeared in a tactical deployment situation—with the PQM-149A designation having been assigned. By January 1992, the Sky Owl was being flown with disc-shaped antennas mounted on *both* of its vertical tail surfaces. *McDonnell Douglas*

version was first demonstrated to the U.S. Army in 1979. Apparently the Army liked what it saw, because it deployed the R4E SkyEye to an active battlefield for testing. A joint Army/Lear Siegler team flew operational R4E surveillance missions in 1984 and 1985 along the Honduran border with Nicaragua from bases at Puerto San Lorenzo and Palmerola. The SkyEyes used low-light-level video systems to track guerilla infiltration along the border. The company also sold SkyEye UAVs to Thailand. The SkyEyes operated by the United States were designated as R4E-40; the Thai variation was identified as R4E-30.

The R4E SkyEye was 12 feet 2 inches long, with a wingspan of 17 feet 7 inches and a launch weight of 520 pounds. It had a nine-hour endurance and could operate at altitudes up to 15,000 feet. It was flown operationally with a variety of reconnaissance

hardware, and there was some discussion of it being used to launch unguided rockets.

A later variation on the SkyEye appeared in the late 1980s during the unmanned aerial vehicle, short range (UAV-SR) competition. The two finalists in this "fly-off" included the McDonnell Douglas Sky Owl—which was a derivative of the Lear Siegler SkyEye—and the Israeli Hunter. The Sky Owl is occasionally mentioned in the same breath with the official Defense Department designation YPQM-149A, but, while this designation was officially reserved for one of the UAV-SR contestants, it was not officially assigned to any aircraft. The YPQM-150A designation was also reserved for the UAV-SR program, but was not assigned. The Hunter was briefly designated as BQM-155A, but it ultimately entered service as the RQ-5.

Army personnel load a Lockheed YMQM-105A Aquila aboard a truck at Fort Huachuca. The glass nose of the YMQM-105A housed a daylight television camera as well as a laser rangefinder/designator and an auto-tracking system. Had the program evolved, the MQM-105B would have been equipped with a gimbaled forward-looking infrared system to give the operational Aquila a night-flight capability. *Lockheed*

The McDonnell Douglas Sky Owl, which made its first flight in June 1991, was 13 feet 5 inches long, with a wingspan of 24 feet. It had an eight-hour endurance and a service ceiling of 15,000 feet. Like the Hunter and the Pioneer, the Sky Owl was constructed with landing gear for takeoffs and landings from runways, but it was also configured for a catapult launch and a parachute recovery. It was radio controlled, but it also had a programmable guidance system. This same system would be revisited in the

LEFT: A technician fine-tunes a Lockheed YMQM-105A Aquila in preparation for a test flight. The rail-launched Aquila was intended to provide the U.S. Army with an easy-to-use UAV for a variety of tasks, including reconnaissance and target designation. *Lockheed*

X-45 UCAV after the McDonnell Douglas UAV team became part of Boeing in 1997.

In June 1992, after a year of flight-testing, the Hunter was chosen over the Sky Owl as the winner of the UAV-SR competition. It would be manufactured in the United States by TRW, which is now a component of the Northrop Grumman Corporation.

Meanwhile, in the United Kingdom, GEC Avionics of Rochester in Kent continued work on yet another twin-boom UAV called Phoenix. Though work on this 4,600-pound UAV had begun in 1982, technical issues led to delays. It was not until 1996 that British Aerospace undertook production of the Phoenix for Her Majesty's armed forces. The Phoenix would first see service in Kosovo in 1999, where its performance was less than stellar.

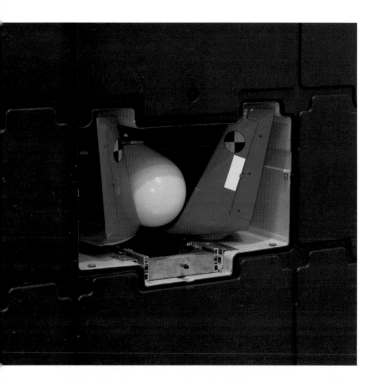

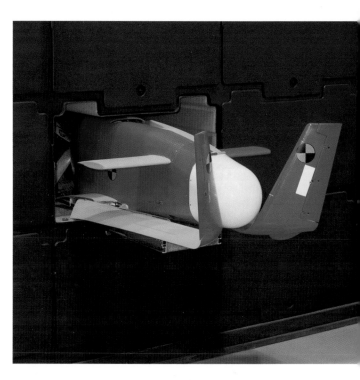

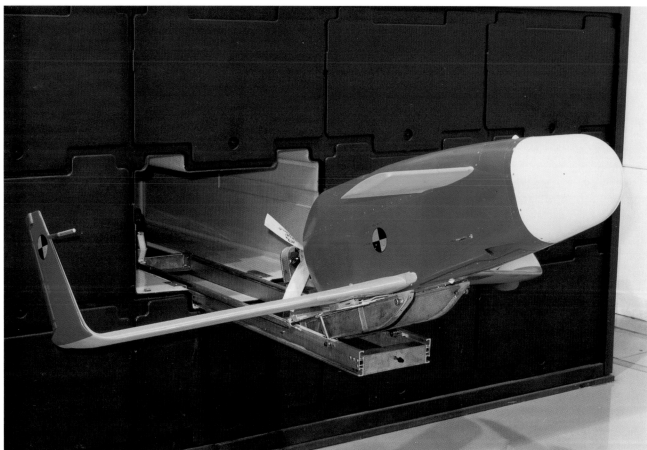

Looking something like the coin lockers at a bus station, or perhaps like a morgue, this is the unique storage module designed for housing Boeing YCQM-121A Pave Tigers. The UAVs were designed to be packed into a 15-locker module and shipped to Central Europe. If World War III had started, they would have been unpacked, unfolded, and launched as a swarm to attack Soviet air defenses. *U.S. Air Force*

Aquila and Pave Tiger

As the U.S. Navy and U.S. Marine Corps looked abroad for what would evolve into the twin-boom, straight-winged Pioneer UAV, the U.S. Army and U.S. Air Force were looking at other configurations. The first major foray by the U.S. Army into American-born small-battlefield UAVs during this era would be the Lockheed MQM-105 Aquila (Eagle) program, which was initiated in the early 1970s under the target acquisition, designation and aerial reconnaissance (TADAR) program. The mission was essentially the same as that for which the Israelis would then be using their Mastiffs and Scouts. Project TADAR was to provide battlefield commanders with a light, easy-to-use observation platform.

However, the U.S. Army *also* wanted to use their drone as an over-the-horizon artillery target designator. The Defense Advanced Research Projects Agency (DARPA) had been working with Ford Aerospace on such a project, code-named *Prairie*, since 1973. The Army wanted this capability incorporated into Aquila so that it could pick targets for their laser-guided Copperhead 155mm artillery shells.

The Lockheed Missiles & Space Company received the full-scale development contract in 1979, and a 17-flight test program involving the YMQM-105 prototype occurred at Fort Huachuca, Arizona, during the summer and fall of 1982. Like the Israeli drones, the Aquila was powered by a single, small gasoline engine driving a pusher propeller, but that is where the similarity in appearance ended. Unlike the Israeli drones, the Aquila had swept wings and no tail. It was 6 feet 10 inches long, with a wingspan of 12 feet 9 inches. The aircraft had no landing gear. It was catapult-launched from a truck and recovered aboard a truck using a large nylon net. It also carried a parachute for emergency landings. The truck recovery system for the Aquila was built in Germany by Dornier, which would have helped make acquisition of the drone system by the German government a potentially attractive proposition.

The Aquila was equipped with a Westinghouse electro-optical payload that included a stabilized laser artillery designator. However, problems with the systems and systems integration led to delays and, ultimately, to the cancellation of the program. The U.S. Army had originally planned to achieve an initial operating capability with the first of 995 MQM-105s by 1985, but this didn't happen, and the program was terminated in 1987. Lockheed's plans for an export version of the Aquila, known as Altair, also died along with the YMQM-105 program.

Like the Army's YMQM-105, the U.S. Air Force YCQM-121 Pave Tiger was a small, compact, tailless drone with swept wings and a pusher propeller. Boeing had initiated the project in-house in 1979 as the BRAVE-200 (Boeing Robotic Air Vehicle). Unlike the contemporary reconnaissance UAVs, BRAVE was an attack drone. Actually, its mission profile made it a cross between a cruise missile and what we would come to expect in a twenty-first-century UCAV. Like a cruise missile, it destroyed its target by running itself into it, but like a UAV, it was recoverable and it could also fly nonlethal missions, such as radar jamming.

In 1983, the Air Force ordered the BRAVE-200 under the designation YCQM-121A, and it was named *Pave Tiger*. The plan at the time was to deploy as many as a thousand of them into Germany by 1987 for defense against a potential Warsaw Pact invasion. The aircraft was just 6 feet 11 inches long, with a wingspan of 8 feet 5 inches. Operationally, the little Tigers would be packed in boxes until use and then launched with a small rocket booster and recovered—if possible—with a parachute.

After limited flight-testing, the Pave Tiger program was cancelled by the United States in 1984. According to the Air Force, the problems in the program were due to "underestimating the complexity" of integrating the airframe and the targeting system. This phrase could easily have been worked into the cancellation explanation for a lot of programs during the Cold War.

Although the U.S. Air Force opted out of the Pave Tiger project, in 1986 the German government was still expressing interest in buying several thousand of them. The Germans continued to look into using the BRAVE-200 as an antiradar system, although that vehicle was competing with the German Messerschmitt-Bolkow-Blohm Tucan UAV. The Pave Tiger concept was revived briefly between 1987 and 1989 as the YCGM-121B, under the Air Force seek spinner program. The improved YCGM-121B (note that the Q for drone had been abandoned) was to have been used to attack enemy radar sites.

Scarab and Peregrine

After the Firebee/Lightning Bug series, Teledyne Ryan continued to develop the concept of the high-speed drone that could be utilized as a reconnaissance platform, although no program would ever match the Firebee family in terms of longevity and volume. However, Teledyne Ryan had abandoned development of such programs by the time Northrop Grumman acquired that company in 1999. The only program of the type that was still current within Northrop Grumman at the turn of the century was the BQM-74 Chukar, which had originated with Northrop's Ventura Division (the former Radioplane), rather than Ryan.

Two of the last of these programs at Teledyne Ryan were the Scarab and Peregrine. Initiated during the 1980s, they were similar airframes for completely different customers. Having delivered Firebees and Lightning Bugs to Israel in the 1970s, Teledyne Ryan was contracted to develop the Model 324 Scarab reconnaissance UAV expressly for Egypt. These turbo-jet-powered UAVs had a top speed of Mach .85 and an endurance of six hours. They were 20 feet long with a wingspan of 11 feet. A total of 56 such aircraft were delivered between 1984 and 1992, and they were assigned to the base at Kom Oshim, south of Cairo.

In 1988, the Department of Defense issued a request for a joint-service UAV that could be either air or surface launched, and that could be used as an

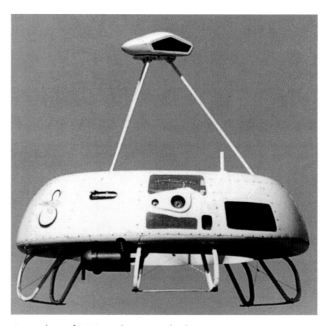

A number of UFO sightings in the late 1980s were probably attributable to Sikorsky's unique Cypher UAV. With its rotor contained entirely within the shroud, the Cypher could push its way through the branches of a tree or other such encumbrances without difficulty, making it an ideal secret-mission platform. *Author collection*

One of the strangest aerodynamic shapes tested in a UAV was that of the Canadair CL-227 Sentinel, seen here during tests aboard a ship at sea. Powered by a Williams WTS34 engine, it stood 54 inches high. It was evaluated by the military services of both Canada and the United States. *Author collection*

aerial target or as a reconnaissance platform. This effort would later be designated as the Unmanned Aerial Vehicle, Medium Range (UAV-MR) program. Under that program, in May 1989, Teledyne Ryan was selected to develop their Model 350, a derivative of the Model 324, under the designation BQM-145A. Known as the Peregrine, the BQM-145A would be powered by a Teledyne Continental F408 turbofan engine. It was 18 feet 4 inches long, with a wingspan of 10 feet 6 inches. As with the Scarab and other such Ryan drones back through the Firebee, it was recoverable by parachute or in midair by helicopters outfitted with MARS. The Peregrine was a pioneer in autonomous operations, being equipped with a preprogrammable flight control system.

The first flight of the YBQM-145A came in May 1992, but the program was canceled 17 months later when both the Navy and Marine Corps dropped out. Only 6 of a planned 500 production Peregrines were built, and they were not flown until 1997.

Drones Without Wings

While many UAV makers were exploring different types of conventional wings for their craft during the 1980s, others were creating rotary-wing vertical-takeoff UAVs that looked nothing like conventional airplanes or helicopters. Indeed, the phrase "unidentified flying object" often comes up in discussions of these strange-looking craft.

The Canadair CL-227 Sentinel had the appearance of two basketballs on top of one another with two contra-rotating propellers between them. These two spherical modules provided favorable surface-to-volume characteristics and reduced radar signature. First test-flown in 1978, the Canadian-made CL-227 stood 54 inches high and had a rotor diameter of 9 feet. Powered by a Williams WTS34 engine, it weighed just 200 pounds empty and was easily portable in a Humvee or a Chinook helicopter.

During the mid-1980s, the CL-227 was tested by the Canadian armed forces, as well as by the U.S. Navy and the U.S. Army. It demonstrated an endurance of four hours, a ceiling of 10,000 feet, and the ability to hover without ground effect at 4,000 feet. The U.S. Army considered fitting it with the laser target designator then being developed for the MQM-105 Aquila.

In England, during the late 1980s, ML Aviation created the Sprite UAV. It was similar to the CL-227, but with a single sphere. Like the CL-227, the Sprite used contra-rotating propellers to achieve stability.

Seen here in a 1991 artist's conception, the Bell Eagle Eye was created for the Department of Defense program known as Tiltrotor Study and Demonstration Unmanned Air Vehicle. The airframe would be built by Burt Rutan's Scaled Composites company. Other Eagle Eye project participants in the 1991 time period included TRW, Honeywell, and Israeli Aircraft Industries (IAI). *Author collection*

This 1994 artist's concept shows how Boeing Heliwings might have looked in an operational situation. The UAVs would be stored in hangars and rolled onto a helipad for launch. The suggestion here is that such operations could have taken place even while a ship was under way in high seas. *Boeing Defense and Space Group*

Rolling out of the hangar at Boeing's facility at Moses Lake in central Washington, the Condor appears wispy and delicate. It also seems small, despite the fact that its wings span 200 feet. These hangars were designed in the 1950s to accommodate the tails of Boeing's B-52s, which were nearly 50 feet tall. *Boeing Historical Services*

A crew prepares the Boeing Condor for a test flight in 1988. As with the great Boeing jet bombers of a past era, the Condor's lengthy wingtips were supported by landing gear. *Boeing Historical Services*

Tested by Sikorsky in the late 1980s and early 1990s, the Cypher UAV was a disk-shaped craft that had the appearance of the classic "flying saucer." Six feet 6 inches in diameter, the Cypher was a 1-foot-thick disk that stood 2 feet tall when parked on its landing brackets. It had a ducted, coaxial rotor completely contained within a composite shroud structure and powered by a 52-horsepower Aldis engine. The shrouded rotor permitted the Cypher to move in tight spaces, such as through tree branches, without the rotor becoming fouled. The shroud also contained a video camera system, the fly-by-wire controls, integrated avionics, and an onboard mission computer. The latter could be equipped with a variety of payloads, such as sensor packages. In flight-tests, the Cypher demonstrated an endurance of up to three hours, and a ceiling of 8,000 feet. During the 1990s, the Cypher was evaluated by the U.S. Army at its urban terrain center at Fort Benning, Georgia, and at the Military Police School at

Fort McClellan, Alabama. The Cypher also flew at the Force Protection Equipment Demonstration in Virginia in 1997.

Eagle Eye and Heliwing

During the late 1980s, as Boeing and Bell Helicopter teamed up to produce the V-22 Osprey "tilt-rotor" heavy lift vertical take off and landing (VTOL) aircraft, both companies were working separately on smaller UAVs based on the same idea. The V-22 Osprey was designed to be the first production rotorcraft that had the capability of taking off vertically like a helicopter and then transitioning to an airplanelike configuration for high-speed forward flight. Bell's Eagle Eye was the first UAV to exploit this same concept.

First flown vertically in 1992, the Eagle Eye is 17 feet 11 inches long with a wingspan of 15 feet 3 inches. During flight-tests at the Yuma Proving Grounds in 1993, the Eagle Eye successfully transitioned between vertical lift and forward flight. In 1998, the Eagle Eye demonstrator aircraft began a 55.5-hour flight-test program, which included 43 landings. During these tests, which were conducted at the Yuma proving ground under a U.S. Navy contract, the UAV reached altitudes up to 14,600 feet and speeds exceeding 230 miles per hour. These tests would lead to the development of a larger-scale Eagle Eye in 2004.

Similar in concept to the Eagle Eye, the Boeing Heliwing was designed to take off vertically, following which the entire aircraft—not just the wing—would rotate for forward flight. Standing on its tail, the Heliwing demonstrator was 7 feet 6 inches tall, and it had a wingspan of 17 feet. The single prototype Heliwing crashed on its sixth test flight in June 1995 as it attempted to rotate to forward flight for the first time.

Condor

One of the most remarkable UAVs of the 1980s was the Boeing Condor, built by Boeing with design input from Dick Rutan, who also designed the *Voyager*, the only airplane to circumnavigate the globe nonstop and unrefueled. As with most of the Rutan aircraft, the Condor was built primarily of carbon fiber composite materials.

With a 200-foot wingspan, greater than that of a 747 jetliner, the Condor was also the largest UAV built up to that time. Its fuselage was 68 feet long, 52 inches high, and 34 inches wide. Its gross weight of 20,000 pounds included 12,000 pounds of fuel

The Boeing Condor is seen here on an early flight, possibly its first, on October 9, 1988. It was built for DARPA's high-altitude, long-endurance (HALE) program, which sought to evaluate extremely high-altitude and extremely long-duration UAVs for possible tactical applications. *Boeing Historical Services*

A Hunter takes off on a mission. Deployed to the Balkans and Iraq, the RQ-5 had amassed over 25,000 flight hours by 2003. After an uncertain start in the mid-1990s, this UAV was supporting U.S. Army division and corps commanders in the early twenty-first century as the service's "interim extended range multi-purpose fixed-wing air vehicle." *Northrop Grumman Media Relations*

Later in its flight-test program, the Boeing Condor was retrofitted with ventral and dorsal radomes and supercharged engines. The big bird would set an altitude record for a propeller aircraft of 67,028 feet in a 1989 flight. *Boeing Historical Services*

The RQ-5 Hunter deployed to the Balkans in 1999 with the U.S. Army's appropriately designated Task Force Hunter. General William David, commander of U.S. forces in Kosovo, described the UAV as "worth its weight in gold." The RQ-5 weighs 1,600 pounds without its rocket booster. *Department of Defense*

and 1,800 pounds of instrumentation. It was powered by a pair of liquid-cooled Teledyne Continental engines, each delivering 175 horsepower. Its Delco Magic flight computers—dinosaurs by today's standard but at that time considered state of the art—were programmed for autonomous operations.

Unknown publicly before its March 1986 rollout was reported in *Aviation Week*, the Condor was a project initiated by DARPA to flight-test an extremely high-altitude UAV with extremely long duration. It was known at the time under the acronym HALE, meaning high-altitude, long-endurance aircraft. The acronym was later shortened to HAE, for high-altitude endurance aircraft.

The huge aircraft made its first flight on October 9, 1988, beginning two years of testing, which was to be conducted from Boeing's large experimental facility at Moses Lake in central Washington State. In the spring of 1989, the Condor set an altitude record for a propeller aircraft of 67,028 feet. Its duration capability was demonstrated to exceed 50 hours, although it was believed capable of staying aloft for several days.

As DARPA intended, the Condor demonstrated the capability for strategic reconnaissance missions with video cameras or film cameras, mapping gear, synthetic aperture radar, and an interface with such other electronic reconnaissance aircraft as the E-3

AWACS or an E-8 Joint Surveillance Target Attack Radar System (J-STARS) aircraft. Such capabilities were said to have made the Condor attractive as an inexpensive alternative to spy satellites, but it is not believed to have been deployed as such. Defensive gear specified for the Condor—if it *had been* deployed on tactical missions—included electronic countermeasures as well as the ability to deploy chaff and flares.

BQM-155/RQ-5 Hunter

The winner of the Defense Department's unmanned aerial vehicle, short range (UAV-SR) competition of 1991–1992, the Hunter was officially ordered in February 1993 under the designation BQM-155A. Designed by the Malat component of IAI, the Hunter would be assembled in the United States by TRW, which has since become a component of Northrop Grumman.

The initial 1993 order was for seven Hunter "systems" of eight aircraft each, and the first of these were delivered to the U.S. Army by April 1995. In the meantime, France and Belgium also each ordered a Hunter system. The Department of Defense had imagined an eventual procurement of as many as 52 systems, but after three crashes in close succession during August and September 1995, the Defense Department decided to terminate the Hunter program

An RQ-2A Pioneer on patrol over a desert landscape. Having served in two Gulf Wars, the Pioneer has certainly had a great deal of combat experience in the desert environment. *Craig Ballard, Pioneer UAV, Inc.*

after the last of the initial seven systems was delivered in December 1996.

Redesignated as RQ-5 after 1997, the Hunter is 22 feet 10 inches long, with a wingspan of 29 feet 2 inches. As with other twin-boom reconnaissance UAVs of Israeli origin, the Hunter has two engines: in this case, two 64-horsepower Moto-Guzzi piston engines. They have an endurance of 12 hours and can operate at altitudes up to 15,000 feet.

Operational gear includes data relay equipment and a dual low-light television (LLTV) and forward-looking infrared (FLIR) installation. Control is by way of a ground-based operator, but the Hunter can be preprogrammed for autonomous operations. The Hunter is equipped with landing gear for runway landings and an arrester hook for short-field landings.

During the late 1990s, the Hunter underwent numerous component quality improvements. For example, failures of the servo actuators, the leading culprit for the 1995 spate of crashes, were identified, and their reliability was increased from 7,800

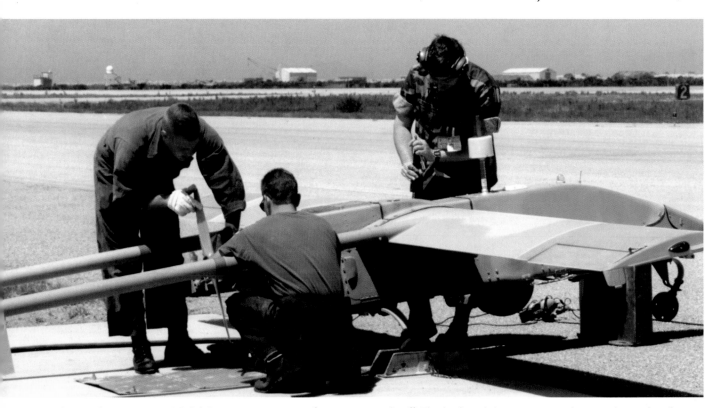

A crew buttons up an RQ-2A Pioneer to prepare it for a runway takeoff. The high-visibility orange markings indicate that this is not going to be a tactical mission. *Craig Ballard, Pioneer UAV, Inc.*

A final check is made of this RQ-2A Pioneer before it is launched. A U.S. Air Force B-1 "Bone" strategic bomber is taxiing in on a parallel runway. *Craig Ballard, Pioneer UAV, Inc.*

IS IT DARPA OR ARPA?

Originally it was ARPA. The Advanced Research Projects Agency (ARPA) was established within the Defense Department on February 7, 1958, "for the direction or performance of such advanced projects in the field of research and development as the Secretary of Defense shall, from time to time, designate by individual project or by category." On March 23, 1972, the name was changed to the Defense Advanced Research Projects Agency (DARPA) and made a separate defense agency under the Office of the Secretary of Defense.

Between February 22, 1993, and February 10, 1996, DARPA was redesignated as ARPA again. With the end of the Cold War, "defense" was being de-emphasized across the board, and the name was changed to keep the agency in line with former president Bill Clinton's strategy paper, titled "Technology for America's Economic Growth, A New Direction to Build Economic Strength."

The agency was again redesignated as DARPA in 1996, and so it remains. To avoid confusion, we have chosen to refer to it as DARPA throughout this work. DARPA can probably be described as the overall most important federal agency in the development of UAVs.

hours to 57,300 hours. Other key components, such as the data link and engine, were examined and upgraded. Before 1995, Hunters were experiencing a mishap rate of 255 per 100,000 hours, but from 1996 to 2001, that rate dropped to 16.

The U.S. Army deployed a contingent of the UAVs to the Balkans in 1999 as the appropriately named Task Force Hunter. They operated extensively in the area, flying routine nighttime reconnaissance missions along the mountainous and heavily wooded Kosovo-Macedonia border, monitoring infiltrations by rebel fighters.

During a June 2001 operation, Hunters maintained surveillance of a U.S. Army convoy as it moved through rebel territory and guided it toward a safe route to the American base. Captain Dan Dittenber, who was with General William David, commander of U.S. forces in Kosovo, as they watched this in real time at the tactical operations center, said later that the general had described the Hunter as "worth its weight in gold." Ironically, a program that had been curtailed because of reliability problems later became a standard of UAV reliability.

A flight deck crew is seen with an RQ-2A Pioneer aboard the amphibious assault ship USS *Tarawa* (LHA-1) in April 1990. *Craig Ballard, Pioneer UAV, Inc.*

The launch stand is secured in preparation for the rocket-assisted takeoff (RATO) of an RQ-2A Pioneer from the deck of the USS *Tarawa* (LHA-1) in April 1990. *Craig Ballard, Pioneer UAV, Inc.*

The huge rail launcher used by Marines ashore for launching RQ-2A Pioneers was brought aboard the USS *Tarawa* (LHA-1) for the series of tests conducted from the ship in April 1990. *Craig Ballard, Pioneer UAV, Inc.*

As an M60 tank lumbers past in the background, these troops are about to launch an RQ-2A Pioneer to scout Iraqi positions in the distance. U.S. Marine Corps Pioneer companies flew 323 missions during Operation Desert Shield and Operation Desert Storm. *Craig Ballard, Pioneer UAV, Inc.*

RQ-2 Pioneer

Originally acquired by the United States in the mid-1980s as an interim UAV, the Pioneer remained in service in the twenty-first century, having been active in the Balkans and in both Gulf Wars. Like the BQM-155/RQ-5 Hunter, the Pioneer is a twin-boom, straight-winged drone with roots in earlier Israeli UAV technology. It is manufactured for the U.S. armed forces by Pioneer UAV, Incorporated, a Maryland-based coventure of Maryland-based AAI Corporation and IAI.

The Pioneer is 16 feet 11 inches long, with a wingspan of 14 feet, and it has a gross weight of 450 pounds and a range of 115 miles. It cruises at 92 miles per hour and has a service ceiling of 15,000 feet and an endurance of up to five and a half hours. It is powered by a 26-horsepower, twin-cylinder, rear-mounted engine driving a pusher propeller.

The Pioneer's surveillance gear centers around a gyro-stabilized, high-resolution MKD-200A LLTV system and an MKD-400C FLIR system for day and night operations, as well as meteorological and chemical detection sensors. It also boasts an integrated radio-relay package for VHF and UHF frequencies. Equipped with landing gear for runway operations, the Pioneer is launched with a rocket-assisted takeoff pack from Navy surface ships, and it can be recovered with a net.

Initially used by the U.S. Navy as a shipboard UAV, the Pioneer has also been operated by the U.S. Marine Corps and the U.S. Army. The first system of eight Pioneer aircraft was delivered to the Navy in July 1986; they shipped out aboard the battleship USS *Iowa* in December of that year. Three systems were delivered to the U.S. Marine Corps in 1987, and one to the U.S. Army at Fort Huachuca, Arizona, in 1990. The Marines assigned part of their Pioneer fleet to ground-based units and part to units assigned to amphibious assault ships.

The Pioneer had its baptism of fire with U.S. forces during Gulf War I, flying long- and short-range patrols. They helped track Iraqi armor in the desert, and they conducted reconnaissance operations in connection with the Marine assault on Faylaka Island. They were operational aboard both the USS *Missouri* and USS *Wisconsin*, providing invaluable target selection and battle-damage assessment in what were probably the last combat deployments by battleships in naval history. When the battleships sent their Pioneers on a low-level surveillance of Faylaka Island after pummeling its defenders with 16-inch gunfire, the surviving Iraqis were observed waving bed sheets in an effort to "surrender" to the UAVs!

Back from a mission over enemy territory during Operation Desert Storm in 1991, this RQ-2A Pioneer will be rapidly refueled, then sent out again. *Craig Ballard, Pioneer UAV, Inc.*

We see here wing calibration as it is done in the field. The RQ-2A Pioneer has proven to be a robust UAV, but bent wingtips, not uncommon in rough landings at remote sites, need to be straightened. *Craig Ballard, Pioneer UAV, Inc.*

Though now grouped as squadrons, the Marine Corps Pioneers were organized into three RPV companies during Gulf War I. The U.S. Army Pioneers were assigned to a UAV platoon attached to VII Corps. For the ground forces, Pioneers were tasked with a variety of missions, especially over-the-horizon tactical reconnaissance and target acquisition.

For all three services, the Pioneer demonstrated outstanding usefulness in the area of battle-damage assessment. They were able to make repeated visits to the same target area, and unlike satellites or high-flying U-2s, they were able to look at targets from different angles. They were especially good at helping commanders ferret out dummy targets.

During Gulf War I, the three Marine Corps Pioneer companies flew 138 missions during Operation Desert Shield (the buildup to the war against Iraq), and 185 missions in Desert Storm (the combat phase of the war), for a total of about 800 hours. The U.S. Army's Pioneer platoon flew 46 sorties averaging 200 minutes each. The U.S. Navy's Pioneers logged 213 hours, providing naval gunfire support on 83 missions. General Walter Boomer, the commander of the Marine Corps expeditionary force, called the Pioneer "the single most valuable intelligence collector" in Gulf War I.

A propeller is attached to a Pioneer UAV prior to a shipboard launch. The men in red are ordnance-men, and the man with the yellow jersey is an aircraft-handling or catapult officer. *Craig Ballard, Pioneer UAV, Inc.*

Clad in his signature yellow jersey, the aircraft-handling officer gives the thumbs-up for a rocket-assisted takeoff from the deck of an *Iowa*-class battleship. The recovery net hangs above the launch site. *Craig Ballard, Pioneer UAV, Inc.*

This dramatic photograph shows an RQ-2A Pioneer just a split second away from impacting into its shipboard recovery net. Because the propeller is on the aft end of the UAV, it won't get fouled in the net. *Craig Ballard, Pioneer UAV, Inc.*

In the wake of the U.S. Navy's questionable decision to phase out its battleships after Gulf War I, the Navy Pioneers were transferred to the landing ship transport dock (LPD) amphibious docking ships. Aboard vessels such as USS *Shreveport*, USS *Denver*, and USS *Austin*, the UAVs would support Marine Expeditionary Units (MEU). Meanwhile, the Marine RPV companies became UAV squadrons, designated as VMUs.

During the early 1990s, the LPD-based Pioneers were active in support of actions in Haiti and Somalia. Navy Pioneers provided surveillance and after-action assessment for joint-service missile tests off the California coast. Pioneers were also detailed to aid the U.S. Border Patrol in antismuggling operations.

The first Pioneer missions over the Balkans involved flights from the USS *Shreveport* over Bosnia and Croatia in October 1995. These included missions to observe the effects of Serbian shelling of the United Nations (UN) sanctuary area at Mostar. In this case,

Pioneers were able to identify which bridges had been destroyed and which had been repaired. The Pioneers from the USS *Shreveport* also surveyed Albania and supported actions ashore by U.S. Navy SEAL teams.

In 1999 and 2000, there was an extensive upgrade to the Pioneer's avionics suite and digital mapping system, as well as to the Common Automatic Recovery System (CARS) used to conduct automatic, hands-off landings on ships, as well as ashore. Theoretically, CARS would permit operations under marginal weather conditions. (The later Pioneers have been given the designation "RQ-2B;" dozens of the original RQ-2As have been upgraded with the RQ-2B–level technology.)

By 2003, as the United States was preparing for Gulf War II, there were nine Pioneer systems on active duty. These included five with the U.S. Navy, one each assigned to the three Marine Corps VMUs, and one to the Joint UAV Training Center (JUAVTC) located at the U.S. Army's Fort Huachuca in Arizona.

This demonstration launch of an RQ-2A Pioneer shows the amount of smoke and fire that accompanies a RATO. *Craig Ballard, Pioneer UAV, Inc.*

Here an RQ-2A Pioneer demonstrates a nearly smokeless RATO using an alternate solid propellant. *Craig Ballard, Pioneer UAV, Inc.*

CHAPTER
THREE

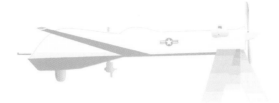

UAVs Come
of Age

By the mid-1990s, the promise and potential of military UAVs to the U.S. armed forces had progressed to the point where they could be considered to be fully integrated into American military doctrine. It had not been easy to arrive at this point. There were many within the American defense establishment who had questioned the value of UAVs as more than just a minor weapon in the arsenal. It was not unlike the prevailing attitude toward aircraft in general during the early years of the twentieth century.

There had been resistance, especially among pilots—for obvious reasons—to the notion of integrating airplanes that *didn't need* pilots into the mix of frontline aircraft. To many, especially pilots of high-performance aircraft, the Hunter and Pioneer looked like toys.

At one time, this bias against taking UAVs seriously as frontline weapons was easily justified. The history of UAVs was filled with technical difficulties, especially with guidance and control, and that perception colored the opinions of many people

in the armed forces. Because of secrecy and compartmentalization, few people still in the service in the 1980s were aware of the full dimensions of the Lightning Bugs, and of the Compass Bin and Buffalo Hunter operations in Southeast Asia.

The paradigm shift had been a long time coming, but by the 1990s it had arrived. In no other country—except Israel, where the value of UAVs in military operations had been recognized a decade earlier—were UAVs embraced with such enthusiasm. By now, the technical capabilities of UAVs had elevated them to the point where they could finally be taken seriously.

In the spring of 1995, a little-known UAV built by General Atomics in San Diego became a surprise hit at the annual Roving Sands joint-training exercise. This UAV, known as the Predator, was soon earmarked for operational deployment to the Balkans.

In July 1995, in a step that was symbolic of the UAV finally coming of age, the U.S. Air Force officially formed its first UAV squadron. General Ronald Fogleman, the Chief of Staff from 1994 to 1997, officially authorized the reactivation of the 11th Reconnaissance Squadron at Indian Springs Auxiliary Airfield in Nevada as a UAV outfit.

The 11th Reconnaissance Squadron was certainly an appropriate squadron. With a lineage dating back

LEFT: With the vast expanse of Rogers Dry Lake in the background, the Lockheed Martin RQ-3 DarkStar is readied for a 1996 test flight on the ramp at the Dryden Flight Research Center. *Denny Lombard, Lockheed Martin Skunk Works*

to 1942, the unit had operated Firebee drones from 1971 until the unit's inactivation in 1979. Between 1991 and 1994, it had been briefly reactivated as an intelligence squadron, but with no aircraft assigned. Because Indian Springs was part of the vast Nellis Air Force Base range, it was located in one of the largest and most restricted military operating areas in the United States. It was a perfect place for the Predators to drill without distraction.

In activating the squadron, Fogleman said, "The bottom line is that the U.S. Air Force will embrace UAVs and work to exploit their potential fully on my watch. We are committed to making UAVs successful contributors to our nation's joint warfighting capability." The rest, as they say, is history.

Introducing the RQ-1/MQ-1 Predator

The airplane that was destined to play the pivotal role in amending both official and public perceptions about the role of UAVs evolved from a contract issued to General Atomics Aeronautical Systems in January 1994. This contract called for a Tier II medium-altitude-endurance (MAE) UAV that would fly reconnaissance missions under U.S. Air Force control on behalf of surface commanders of all the services. As with other UAVs of the early 1990s, such as the DarkStar and Global Hawk, the Predator program was an Advanced Concept Technology Demonstration (ACTD) program, although it was the first such demonstrator of its generation to evolve into an operational aircraft.

The first flight of the Predator prototype occurred in June 1994, and early aircraft were demonstrated at the Roving Sands 95 air defense exercise in April and May 1995. The Predators performed so well in this stateside demonstration that the decision was made to use them as the centerpiece of the Air Force's first UAV squadron and deploy them overseas to the Balkans in July 1995.

The Predator was the first aircraft to be designated after the Defense Department reactivated the "Q for drone" designation prefix. Because it was a reconnaissance aircraft, it became the RQ-1. When Predators were armed in 2001, they became multimission aircraft and were redesignated as MQ-1s. Often, unarmed Predators are still referred to as RQ-1s, but all armed Predators are technically MQ-1s.

The RQ-1/MQ-1 Predator is 27 feet long, stands 6 feet 11 inches tall on its tricycle landing gear, and has a wingspan of 48 feet 8 inches. The landing gear permits runway operations. It weighs 1,130 pounds empty, and has a maximum takeoff weight of 2,250 pounds and a payload capacity of 450 pounds. The Predator cruises at between 85 and 135 miles per hour. It has a range of 450 miles and a service ceiling of 25,000 feet, with an endurance of about 40 hours, depending on configuration and cruising speed.

In this digital image, the RQ-1 that conducted a simulated Navy aerial reconnaissance flight with the battle group of the aircraft carrier USS *Carl Vinson* (CVN-70) in December 1995 provided real-time infrared and color video to intelligence analysts and controllers aboard the ship. *Department of Defense—Petty Officer 3rd Class Jeffrey Viano, U.S. Navy*

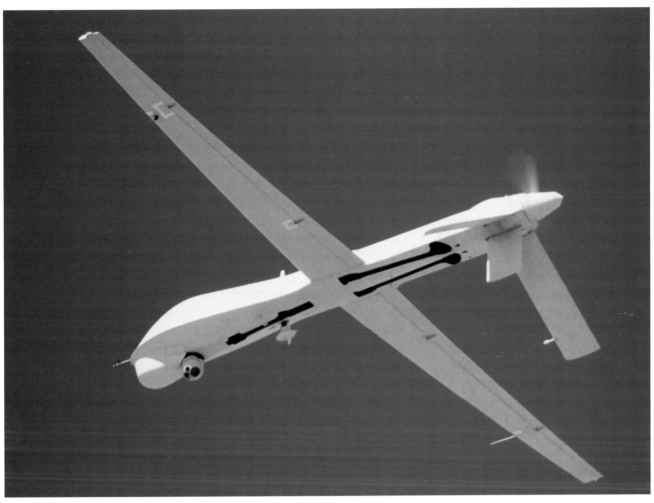

This March 2000 bottom view of the General Atomics RQ-1 Predator provides a good look at the Lynx side aperture radar and the 14-inch Skyball gimbal. *General Atomics Aeronautical Systems*

In this view, we see the General Atomics RQ-1 Predator with the dark stripes of the optional deicing system on the leading edges of the wings. *General Atomics Aeronautical Systems*

Seen here over the USS *Tarawa* amphibious assault ship in November 1997 is a General Atomics Gnat-750, the precursor to the Predator. The "pilot" is aboard the ship. *General Atomics Aeronautical Systems*

The General Atomics I-Gnat is an improved version of the original Gnat-750 and is designed to take off and land conventionally from any hard surface. *General Atomics Aeronautical Systems*

The Predator is powered by a Rotax four-cylinder engine. Founded in Germany in 1920, Rotax has been owned by the Bombardier company of Canada since 1970. Rotax makes small piston engines for a variety of applications, from boats and motorcycles to light aircraft, and is perhaps best known in North America for its snowmobile engines.

Among other payload options, the Predator is equipped with the Northrop Grumman TESAR synthetic-aperture radar (SAR) with 1-foot resolution and all-weather reconnaissance capability. It can also fly with a laser designator and rangefinder, as well as electronic support and countermeasures gear and a moving target indicator (MTI). The Raytheon multi-spectral targeting system (MTS) provides real-time imagery. The television system is equipped with a variable zoom and a telescopic spotter. These "eyes" of the surveillance gear are contained in a Versatron/Wescam electro-optical Skyball gimbal located in the "chin" of the aircraft. Because it contains the laser target designator,

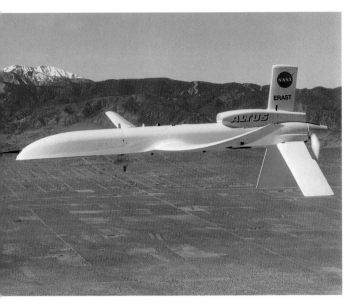

Seen here over the California foothills in June 1998, the General Atomics Altus II was operated by NASA as part of its Environmental Research Aircraft and Sensor Technology (ERAST) program. *General Atomics Aeronautical Systems*

During tests in August 1999, the General Atomics Prowler II tactical UAV demonstrated an endurance of 18 hours. The Prowler is a scaled-down variation on the Gnat. *General Atomics Aeronautical Systems*

crews call this spherical turret a "laser ball." The Predator has UHF and VHF radio relay links, a C-band line-of-sight data link, and Ku-band satellite data links.

As with other UAVs, Predators are acquired and delivered as multiaircraft systems. In the case of the RQ-1, the system includes four aircraft, a ground-control station in a 30-foot trailer, and a Trojan Spirit data distribution terminal equipped with an 18-foot satellite dish for Ku-band transmissions.

By February 2004, the 100th Predator had been delivered to the U.S. Air Force. Meanwhile, the Italian air force had ordered six from General Atomics in August 2001. Of these, five would be assembled in Italy by Meteor company. Predators are operated by France under the name Horus.

Reactivated in July 1995, the 11th Reconnaissance Squadron was the first Air Force field unit to operate the Predator. The second Predator unit, the 15th Reconnaissance Squadron, began flying the RQ-1 in August 1997. A third unit, the 17th Reconnaissance Squadron, was activated in March 2002. All three are headquartered at Indian Springs Auxiliary Airfield, but they have been frequently deployed to numerous overseas "hot zones."

Designated as Operation Nomad Vigil, the first operational deployment of the Predator overseas occurred between July and November 1995 in support of the joint operation over Bosnia known as Provide Promise. Assigned to the U.S. European Command, and under U.S. Army administrative control, the Predators were based at Gjader in Albania.

During this deployment, Predators also flew in support of Operation Deliberate Force. This was the NATO air campaign against Serbian forces that overran the UN "safe zone" at Srebrenica in Bosnia and perpetrated what has been called the worst case of mass murder of civilians to occur in Europe since World War II. In their baptism of fire, Predators flew 52 missions. Two were lost: one was destroyed by Serbian antiaircraft fire, and the other was destroyed by its operators to keep it from falling into enemy hands.

Nomad Vigil was followed in March 1996 by Nomad Endeavor, which was an element of NATO's Operation Joint Endeavor. Based at Taszar, Hungary, Predators flew an average of six missions a week—weather permitting. These continued through Joint Endeavor, which ended in December 1996, and Operation Joint Guard, which ended in June 1998. Weather, which is very severe in the Balkans in wintertime, was an issue, and it led to modifications to the RQ-1s, including deicing gear.

In April 1997, when Pope John Paul II made his historic visit to war-torn Bosnia, a Predator from the 11th Reconnaissance Squadron flew two dedicated security surveillance missions totaling 22.5 hours. On April 11, the first day of the papal visit, the Predator was the only aircraft to provide real-time imagery.

During the summer of 1998, the Balkan situation heated up once again. There was considerable fighting between ethnic Albanian separatists and the ethnic Serbian army of what was left of Yugoslavia in Yugoslav-occupied Kosovo. In October, a cease-fire was declared in accordance with the UN Security Council Resolution 1199 of September 23. NATO initiated Operation Eagle Eye to monitor this cease-fire. The Taszar-based Predators of the 11th Reconnaissance Squadron became an integral part of this operation.

By January 1999, the Kosovo cease-fire had collapsed, and there was widespread fighting, mainly initiated by Serbian forces. At a peace conference held in Paris, the Serbian delegation refused to accept a peaceful settlement to the conflict, so NATO undertook Operation Allied Force to compel compliance with Resolution 1199. On March 24, NATO aircraft began a three-month air offensive against Yugoslavia. The major contribution to this

A sunrise view shows Lockheed Martin Skunk Works personnel checking out the RQ-3 DarkStar. The Tier III Minus aircraft was built at the company's facility at Palmdale, in California's Mojave Desert. *Lockheed Martin*

The Lockheed Martin RQ-3 DarkStar Tier III Minus UAV, seen in this marvelous illustration by Billy Smallwood, was a large, futuristic stealth aircraft. *U.S. Air Force—Billy Smallwood*

offensive was by the United States under Operation Noble Anvil.

By the time Operation Allied Force began, there were no longer RQ-1 Predators in the region, but the 11th Reconnaissance Squadron was rapidly redeployed to the Balkans. This time, their operating location was the U.S. Army's Eagle Base, near Tuzla, Bosnia. Meanwhile, the U.S. Navy also committed UAVs to the Allied Force/Noble Anvil action. However, the RQ-2 Pioneers operating from ships in the Mediterranean were not able to operate in the severe winter weather, and they were withdrawn from action.

The Predators conducted surveillance and battle-damage assessment missions through the end of the air campaign on June 10. Two of them were shot down by hostile ground fire, and one was lost due to a fuel system malfunction. After the end of Allied Force/Noble Anvil, the 11th Reconnaissance Squadron remained in Tuzla for several months during the summer of 1999, and they returned to Tuzla for periodic deployments in 2000 and early 2001.

When not being used, the Predators are disassembled and stored at Indian Springs in crates that are called "coffins." In turn, these are packed in what airmen refer to, naturally, as the "morgue." At the time of a deployment, the coffins are pulled from the morgue and airlifted to the forward operating base for reassembly.

For all their tactical success, the Predators had been experiencing a great many teething problems during the Balkan deployment. By September 2001, on the eve of deployment to southwest Asia, 19 of the 68 Predators that had been delivered had been lost. Four were confirmed lost in the Balkans, while the rest were lost mainly due to operator error. In a September 2001 briefing, a Senior Defense Department official, who declined to be named, confirmed that, "A good number of them were lost [due to] operator error. It's hard to land this thing. The

The Lockheed Martin RQ-3 DarkStar is towed out of the hangar at the Dryden Flight Research Center at Edwards Air Force Base in California, in preparation for a test flight. *Carol Dodd, Lockheed Martin Skunk Works*

The Lockheed Martin RQ-3 DarkStar lifts off autonomously for its debut flight at the Dryden Flight Research Center at Edwards Air Force Base on the morning of March 29, 1996. *Lockheed Martin*

Seen here in June 1998, the second RQ-3 Tier III Minus DarkStar UAV makes a fully autonomous touchdown approach at NASA's Dryden Flight Research Center using the differential global positioning system (GPS). *NASA—Carla Thomas*

Soaring high above the Mojave Desert, the RQ-3 DarkStar reached an altitude of 5,000 feet on its 20-minute first flight in March 1996. *Lockheed Martin*

operator has the camera pointing out the front of the plane, but he really has lost a lot of situational awareness that a normal pilot would have of where the ground is and where the attitude of his aircraft is, . . . so we have a lot of losses just from hitting the ground."

Though the Predator would eventually evolve into a potent—even legendary—weapon, there were still a great many misgivings about its performance after the experience with it in the Balkans. A report issued in early 2001 by the Pentagon's operational test

and evaluation office had criticized the Predator for being vulnerable to weather conditions, "including visible moisture such as rain, snow, ice, frost or fog."

Based on the combat experience in the Balkan conflicts, the Air Force and General Atomics had undertaken a Block 1 Predator Upgrade program in May 1998. Included in this upgrade package was the capability for continuous coverage over "areas of interest" without any loss of time on station, secure air-traffic-control voice relay, Ku-band satellite tuning, and implementation of an Air Force Mission Support System (AFMSS). The improved Predator would be equipped with a more powerful turbocharged Rotax 914 engine and wing-deicing systems to facilitate cold-weather operations. The service ceiling was increased to 45,000 feet, and the payload expanded to 750 pounds.

The expanded capabilities resulted in the RQ-1B Predator, which is not to be confused with the MQ-9A Predator B. The RQ-1B first entered service in April 2001 during action on the border between Yugoslavia and Macedonia. Officially, the *B* designation refers to the entire updated Predator "system," including the aircraft and its ground equipment, and the air vehicles are officially known to the Air Force as RQ-1Ls or MQ-1Ls (the version of the RQ-1L armed with Hellfire missiles). The aircraft of the earlier RQ-1A system are officially RQ-1Ks.

The Tier II Plus Northrop Grumman RQ-4 Global Hawk UAV, seen here in a dramatic illustration by Virginia Reyes, would revolutionize long-endurance, high-altitude reconnaissance during the conflicts at the dawn of the twenty-first century. *U.S. Air Force—Virginia Reyes*

Predators had flown more than 600 active combat missions in the Balkans. These were merely a prelude to what awaited them in the twenty-first century.

WHAT IS A UAV "SYSTEM"?

The term *system* has been used by the U.S. Defense Department to refer to the way operational UAVs are acquired and deployed. Rather than being ordered as individual aircraft, they are ordered as systems. A system includes a certain number of aircraft, such as eight in the case of the RQ-2 Pioneer or RQ-5 Hunter, or four in the case of the RQ-1 Predator, plus support equipment.

In addition to the aircraft, each system also contains such items as ground-control shelters, a mission-planning shelter, a launch-and-recovery shelter, ground-data terminals, remote-video terminals, modular mission payload modules (at least one for each aircraft), and air data relays, in addition to miscellaneous launch, recovery, and ground-support equipment.

Gnat and Prowler

No discussion of the General Atomics Predator UAV is complete without a mention of the company's less-well-known Gnat-750, the predecessor to Predator. The Gnat has its roots in the top-secret Amber project that dates back to 1984. In that year,

DARPA contracted with the Leading Systems company of Irvine, California, to build a long-endurance UAV under the code name "Amber." The plan was for the same basic airframe design to be adapted for use as a reconnaissance aircraft and as a cruise missile.

First flown in November 1986, Amber had the general appearance—including the V-tail and pusher propeller—of the later Predator. It was 15 feet long, with a wingspan of 28 feet, and was powered by a four-cylinder piston engine. Like the Predator and the Gnat, Amber was made of composite materials. During flight-tests in 1987, Amber demonstrated an endurance of at least 24 hours. DARPA and the U.S. Navy (the service most interested in the project) continued to study the aircraft through the end of the decade. The Amber I, an "evolved" reconnaissance version, made its debut flight in October 1989. Approximately 13 Amber or Amber I vehicles had been built by 1990, when the program was canceled for budgetary reasons.

In the meantime, Leading Systems was working on the Gnat-750, a simpler export version of Amber that first flew in 1989. After General Atomics acquired Leading Systems in 1990, the Gnat-750 project continued. Both the Turkish government and the U.S. Central Intelligence Agency (CIA) expressed interest in the Gnat's capabilities. The CIA went so far as to deploy the Gnat-750 to Albania in 1994 for surveillance operations over the

The first Global Hawk turns in for a landing on the main runway at Edwards Air Force Base in California at the end of its debut flight on February 28, 1998. By this time, the Department of Defense was already touting the fact that the Global Hawk could operate at altitudes up to 65,000 feet and remain on station for 24 hours. The first flight was considerably shorter than that. *Department of Defense*

imploding Yugoslavia. These would be withdrawn in favor of the more capable Predator, but improved Gnat-750s were redeployed to the Balkans by the CIA under the appropriate operational code name *Lofty View*.

Still in production in the twenty-first century, the Gnat-750 is also operated by various U.S. and international customers, including the U.S. Department of Energy, which uses it for atmospheric monitoring. The Gnat-750 is 16 feet 5 inches long, with a wingspan of 35 feet 4 inches. It has a proven service ceiling of 25,000 feet and an endurance of 40 hours. The newer, high-altitude I-Gnat is 21 feet long with a wingspan of 42 feet. Power for the Gnats is delivered by a single Rotax 912 engine.

During the G-8 Summit conference at Kananaskis, Alberta, during the summer of 2002, General Atomics was called upon to provide surveillance using its I-Gnat aircraft. Configured with a synthetic-aperture radar (SAR) and optical sensors, the UAV provided real-time intelligence information to support the Canadian security efforts. The Canadian Armed Forces also integrated the I-Gnat into a field-training

exercise called Robust Ram, which was held in Suffield, Alberta.

The Prowler II was a scaled-down version of the Gnat that was 13 feet 11 inches long, with a wingspan of 24 feet. Designed to meet tactical UAV performance requirements, it had an endurance of more than 18 hours and a payload capacity of 100 pounds. It was also designed to use the same ground-control station and data link as both the Predator and the Gnat.

Altus

Another variation on the Predator, developed by General Atomics Aeronautical Systems, was the Altus UAV, which was designed for high-altitude, long-duration scientific sampling missions. Altus I was flown for the Department of Energy and the Sandia National Laboratory by the Naval Postgraduate School. The plan had been to use its high-altitude capabilities to further atmospheric research and to study hurricane patterns. The Altus I aircraft flew several developmental test flights from Rogers Dry Lake adjacent to NASA's Dryden Flight

In April 2000 the fourth RQ-4 Global Hawk deployed from Edwards Air Force Base in California to Eglin Air Force Base in Florida for six weeks. The aircraft made the transcontinental flight nonstop, setting a UAV endurance record of 31.5 hours nonstop. While deployed to Eglin Air Force Base, the vehicle would participate in two exercises. *U.S. Air Force—George Rohlmaller*

Research Center at Edwards Air Force Base, California, during August 1997. On its final flight, it reached an altitude of 43,500 feet.

Altus II was built for NASA's Environmental Research Aircraft and Sensor Technology (ERAST) program. Both aircraft were powered by turbocharged piston engines: Altus I by a single-stage turbocharger, and Altus II by a two-stage turbocharger to enable it to fly at altitudes in the 65,000-foot environment. The two aircraft were each 22 feet long and had a wingspan of 55 feet.

In May 2001, the Altus II was flown with the "FiRE" payload over wildfires in southern California in a test cosponsored by NASA and the U.S. Forest Service. The objective was to demonstrate that a UAV could be used to collect thermal infrared data and to serve as an effective fire fighting tool. The

Altus II was equipped with the airborne infrared disaster assessment system (AIDAS) to measure fire intensity and send diagnostic images to firefighters on the ground in near real time.

Newer Small UAVs

Toward the end of the twentieth century, the U.S. armed forces continued to look into reconnaissance and target-acquisition UAVs that were in the same size and weight class, or smaller than, the Hunter or Pioneer. Among these systems was the Sparrow Hawk, a VTOL UAV, developed as a "Rapid Prototyping" experiment in the early 1990s by what was then the McDonnell Douglas Astronautics Company in St. Louis.

Powered by a single propeller, the Sparrow Hawk was unusual because it was controlled using only aerodynamic control surfaces. This aerodynamic

control scheme even handled engine torque and propeller swirl during takeoff and landing. Concept validation wind-tunnel testing was done in the McDonnell Douglas low-speed wind-tunnel facilities in St. Louis, and early subscale flight-tests were done at the Sky Technology facilities in Texas. The full-scale development flight demonstration tests were done at the U.S. Army's closed-range facility in Arizona.

Two more recent systems that received official Department of Defense drone designations are the RQ-6 Outrider and the RQ-7 Shadow. The Outrider program began in 1996 with the notion of developing a multiservice UAV for reconnaissance and target acquisition that was smaller than the Hunter and Pioneer UAVs. It was intended that the aircraft and its control equipment be compact enough to be portable by two vehicles the size of a Humvee, or by a single C-130.

Built by Alliant Techsystems, the Outrider was 9 feet 11 inches long and weighed 385 pounds.

U.S. Air Force technicians from the 31st Test and Evaluation Squadron, based at Edwards Air Force Base, prep the fourth RQ-4 Global Hawk prior to a mission flown from Eglin Air Force Base in June 2000. The vehicle reached 64,500 feet in one 22-hour mission during this Joint Task Force exercise. *U.S. Air Force—Bobbi Garcia*

A new Global Hawk test aircraft arrives at Edwards Air Force Base after its delivery flight. The new arrival joins the other Global Hawk UAVs undergoing flight-testing as part of the engineering, manufacturing, and development phase of defense acquisition. The new aircraft's first flight went exactly as planned, said Lieutenant Colonel Michael Guidry, director of the Global Vigilance Combined Test Force. "This new aircraft will help us support quick-reaction testing of the Global Hawk," Guidry said. "Based on requests we get from the field, we can incorporate real-time changes to the aircraft. This allows our test force to develop a better weapon system for everyone who takes it into combat." *Department of Defense—Carlos Rolon*

Sensors onboard the Northrop Grumman RQ-4 Global Hawk can provide near-real-time imagery of an "area of interest" to the battlefield commander via worldwide satellite communication links and the system's ground segment. *Northrop Grumman Media Relations*

This photo taken at Edwards Air Force Base in 2003 provides a good "portrait" view of a Northrop Grumman RQ-4 Global Hawk in its operational gray livery. The radome cover remains white to reflect solar radiation at high altitude. *Northrop Grumman Media Relations*

Featuring a joined twin-wing design for high lift and low drag, it had a wingspan of 11 feet. The powerplant was a McCulloch 4318F four-cylinder engine driving a pusher propeller. It had an endurance in excess of 10 hours and a service ceiling of 15,000 feet. The Outrider was designed to operate from unprepared landing strips or U.S. Navy assault ships.

During a 185-flight-test program, the Outrider did not measure up to expectations, and both the U.S. Navy and Marine Corps withdrew the Outrider from consideration. The Army gave the aircraft one last chance, entering it in the fly-off at Fort Huachuca, Arizona, aimed at picking an aircraft for the Tactical UAV (TUAV) requirement. The fly-off, which was conducted during October and November 1999, featured four aircraft. In addition to the Outrider, these were the General Atomics Prowler II, the TRW Sentry, and the AAI Shadow 200. The winner, announced in December 1999, was the Shadow 200, which was ordered into production as the RQ-7.

The RQ-7 is a twin-boom aircraft based on AAI's successful RQ-2 Pioneer UAV. It is 11 feet long with a wingspan of 12 feet 9 inches. It has a gross weight at takeoff of 327 pounds and is designed to carry a payload of about 50 pounds. The powerplant is an AR741 rotary engine. Designed to be launched from a hydraulic launcher, the Shadow is equipped with a tricycle landing gear for runway landings. Full-rate production of nine systems of four aircraft each was ordered in December 2002.

On its own initiative, AAI built the Shadow 400, which is a potential shipboard variation on the Shadow 200. The Shadow 400 features the tactical

radar (TUAVR) system developed by Northrop Grumman from the AN/ZPQ-1 Tactical Endurance Aperture Radar (TESAR) used on the U.S. Air Force Predator. Slightly larger than the RQ-7, the Shadow 400 is 12 feet 6 inches long, with a wingspan of 16 feet 10 inches and a gross weight of 442 pounds. It has an endurance of five hours.

Even larger, AAI's multipayload Shadow 600 is 15 feet 8 inches long, with a wingspan of 22 feet 3 inches. It has a gross weight of 583 pounds and an endurance of up to 14 hours. The engine is the 52-horsepower AR801.

High Altitude Drones

By the early 1990s, the U.S. defense establishment was ready to accept UAVs as a permanent class of military aircraft, with a necessary and defined role. Against this backdrop, the DarkStar was a pioneering aircraft. It opened a new era in defense procurement and in the way the Defense Department approached UAVs conceptually.

In 1993, DARPA had initiated its HAE UAV advanced airborne reconnaissance program. HAE was a successor to the agency's HALE program of the 1980s that had led to the development of the Boeing Condor.

HAE was also an ACTD program developed outside the traditional defense acquisition system, and the law imposed the standards and minimum system requirements. In was the first project executed under Section 845 of Public Law 103-160, Section 845, which gave DARPA broad authority to carry out prototype projects that are directly relevant to weapons or

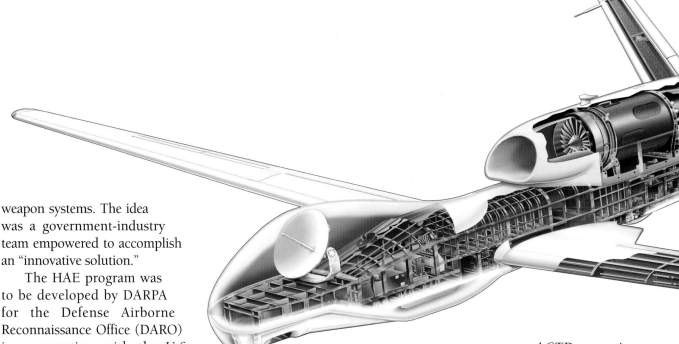

weapon systems. The idea was a government-industry team empowered to accomplish an "innovative solution."

The HAE program was to be developed by DARPA for the Defense Airborne Reconnaissance Office (DARO) in cooperation with the U.S. Army, U.S. Navy, and U.S. Air Force. It would involve two complementary aircraft, the Tier II Plus and the Tier III Minus. Named DarkStar, the Tier III Minus aircraft would eventually be designated as the RQ-3, while the Tier II Plus aircraft, named Global Hawk, would be designated as RQ-4. Tier III Minus was on a faster development track and received the lower Reconnaissance Drone RQ designation number.

The two HAE ships would be designed to interface with a common mission ground-control station. The payload systems for both would include SAR and Electro-Optical/Infrared (EO/IR) sensors.

As precursors to the twenty-first-century generation of UAVs, the DarkStar and Global Hawk were to be designed with completely programmable control systems for autonomous operations from takeoff to landing. The automated controls would use the differential global positioning system (GPS).

The types differed in that the Tier II Plus was to be defined by extremely long endurance, while the Tier III Minus was optimized for a more moderate endurance, but it had low-observable, or "stealth," characteristics for operating in a high-threat environment. Both tiers were seen as having a role to play in possible future tactical scenarios.

RQ-3 DarkStar

In July 1994, Lockheed Martin was awarded the contract for the DarkStar, the first Section 845

ACTD project. Lockheed's Skunk Works was responsible for the design and development of the fuselage, subsystems, final assembly, and systems integration. Boeing, the principal subcontractor, would have responsibility for the wing and for wing subsystem development and testing. Together, Lockheed Martin and Boeing completed the first RQ-3 aircraft in less than a year. The DarkStar prototype rolled out at the Skunk Works facility at Palmdale, California, on June 1, 1995.

Resembling a "flying saucer" from the front, the DarkStar's airframe was composed primarily of nonmetal composites, and it had no vertical tail surfaces. It was only 15 feet from front to back, but its wing spanned 69 feet. The DarkStar had a gross weight of 8,600 pounds and was powered by a single Williams FJ-44-1 turbofan engine. It was rated with a top speed of 345 miles per hour, with an endurance of 12.7 hours, or 8 hours above 45,000 feet. It had a service ceiling of 50,000 feet. As with most modern UAVs conceived since the 1980s, the DarkStar was equipped with conventional landing gear for runway operations.

From Palmdale, the DarkStar prototype was transported to the Air Force Flight Test Center at nearby Edwards Air Force Base, where it had been scheduled to fly late in 1995 until taxi tests uncovered some potential control problems. The first DarkStar made its debut flight on March 29, 1996. Taking off autonomously at 6:25 a.m. for a

The remarkably detailed illustration shows the internal structure of the Northrop Grumman RQ-4 Global Hawk. Note the electro-optical/infrared (EO/IR) and synthetic aperture radar (SAR) systems, as well as the Rolls Royce-Allison AE3007H turbofan engine. *Northrop Grumman*

20-minute flight, the DarkStar completed a preprogrammed routine of basic flight maneuvers and reached an altitude of about 5,000 feet. Harry Berman, the DARPA program manager and former chief systems engineer for the Boeing Condor program, commented, "This marks a major milestone in the progress of the program. The entire team from Lockheed and Boeing has done an excellent job."

By this time, the second DarkStar prototype was nearing completion at Palmdale and was nearly ready to join the flight-test program. Meanwhile, the first RQ-4 Global Hawk was nearing completion, and there was talk of a first flight before the end of the year. However, the HAE program was about to be dealt a blow that would delay it until 1998.

The second flight of the first DarkStar aircraft did not go so well. On April 22, 1996, less than a month after the first flight, the first DarkStar was scheduled for a nearly three-hour mission, but it encountered problems just as it took off. The main gear lifted off the runway before the nose wheel lifted off, and the aircraft experienced a series of pitch oscillations. Ten seconds after it cleared the runway, the DarkStar rolled to the left and crashed in a ball of fire. The composite structure was almost completely destroyed.

Despite this, there was still keen interest in both of the HAE programs. In April 1997, Charles Heber, DARPA's HAE director, told the Senate Armed Services Committee that the Joint Requirements Oversight Council of the Joint Chiefs of Staff "strongly recommends pursuing both the Global Hawk and DarkStar systems."

After 26 months of reworking the system, the second DarkStar made a 44-minute fully autonomous first flight on June 29, 1998. The second DarkStar had been modified with new landing gear and redesigned flight control software. Intensive simulations had started in March 1998, before the taxi tests. Harry Berman summed it up by saying that the team had "worked hard over the past two years to determine the cause of the mishap and make system-wide improvements in the robustness of the aircraft and ground system. The resumption of flight-tests puts the program back on track."

The track would be a short one. After five successful flights by the second DarkStar, the Defense Department officially terminated the Tier III Minus program on January 29, 1999. By that time, it seemed that there was more interest in the potential usefulness of the long-range Global Hawk than the stealthy DarkStar. However, Skunk Works was already at work on a supersecret successor to the RQ-3. Though it was not officially acknowledged at the time, this highly capable "Son of DarkStar" would see action during Gulf War II in 2003.

THE THREE TIERS OF UAV

During the 1990s, the U.S. Department of Defense used a multitier classification system to group its UAV fleet into broad categories, based on their altitude and endurance capabilities. The system is no longer as commonly used in official documents as it was then.

Tier I describes tactical UAVs operating at altitudes up to 15,000 feet, with a range up to 150 miles and an endurance of between 5 and 24 hours. An example would be the RQ-2 Pioneer.

Tier II UAVs operate at altitudes between 3,000 feet to 25,000 feet, have a range of up to 550 miles, and have an endurance exceeding 24 hours. The RQ-1 Predator is a Tier II UAV.

Tier II Plus identifies a strategic UAV operating at altitudes up to 65,000 feet, with a range of 3,000 miles. These are also referred to by the acronym HAE (high altitude endurance), which was formerly HALE (high-altitude, long-endurance). The RQ-4 Global Hawk, which has demonstrated an endurance exceeding 40 hours, is an example of a Tier II Plus HAE aircraft.

Tier III Minus UAVs are strategic HAE vehicles, such as the RQ-3 DarkStar, that also embody stealth or low-observable characteristics, and have a shorter endurance than the Tier II Plus.

The Tiers were used to refer to the entire system, including ground control, and not just the specific aircraft, although it was natural that the Tier designations came to be used interchangeably with aircraft names and designations.

RQ-4 Global Hawk

Developed at roughly the same time as its HAE stablemate, the DarkStar, the Global Hawk was initiated in 1995 as a Tier II Plus advanced concept technology demonstrator to assess the utility of such vehicles—but the aircraft unexpectedly found itself at war far sooner than had been envisioned.

The largest military UAV known to be operational at the turn of the century, the U.S. Air Force's big RQ-4 Global Hawk is in roughly the same size class as the manned Lockheed U-2 and the Compass Cope prototypes of a quarter century earlier. It is also more than twice the size of the DarkStar. The Global Hawk is 44 feet long, with a wingspan of 116 feet. It weighs 25,600 pounds when fully fueled and has a range of 13,000 miles. The fuselage is constructed of aluminum, but fiberglass composites

have been used for the wings, wing fairings, empennage, engine cover, engine intake, and the three radomes. The powerplant is a single Rolls Royce-Allison AE3007H turbofan, delivering 7,600 pounds of thrust.

The Global Hawk's endurance was originally listed as 24 hours, although it has often exceeded this during operational deployments. With their pre-programmable controls, Global Hawks can take off autonomously, fly halfway around the world, and land without an operator on the ground doing anything more than monitoring its systems remotely.

Since the United States began military operations in the global war on terrorism in October 2001, Global Hawks have been deployed to provide the battlefield commanders of all the services with near-real-time, high-resolution intelligence, surveillance, and reconnaissance imagery. Its long endurance also permits the aircraft to view and track moving targets for long periods of time.

Cruising at altitudes up to 65,000 feet, Global Hawks can survey large geographic areas at better than 3-foot resolution, and are capable of forming 1,900 1-foot spot images at 1-foot resolution. With its cloud-penetrating EO/IR and SAR systems, an RQ-4 can cover an area the size of Illinois on a single mission. A broad area maritime surveillance system has subsequently been added to the RQ-4's capabilities portfolio, permitting the UAV and its sensor package to be controlled from a ship.

Manufactured by Teledyne Ryan, which was absorbed by Northrop Grumman in 1999, the Global Hawk prototype rolled out in San Diego in February 1997. The first flight occurred at Edwards Air Force Base on February 28, 1998. Initial orders called for the U.S. Air Force to acquire 51 Global Hawks, and the first six of these were delivered through the end of 2002. Though the Global Hawk was initiated as an Air Force program, the U.S. Navy and the armed services of Australia, Germany, and Japan have expressed interest in adding the big UAVs to their fleets.

Starting in June 1999, the Global Hawk was evaluated in a series of Joint Forces Command exercises. In April 2000, the fourth Global Hawk aircraft was deployed to Eglin Air Force Base in Florida for a series of operations that would include the first trans-Atlantic RQ-4 flight. In February 2001, the Global Hawk became the first UAV to be awarded the Collier Trophy for aeronautical achievement by the National Aeronautic Association.

The AAI RQ-7 Shadow 200 clearly shares many features with its larger precursor, the RQ-2 Pioneer. It is, however, 6 feet shorter than the Pioneer, and it has a 2-foot-shorter wingspan. *Author collection*

The McDonnell Douglas Sparrow Hawk is seen here during flight-testing in May 1992. It was a "tail sitter" VTOL UAV that was developed in a "Rapid Prototyping" demonstration. *McDonnell Douglas*

Pathfinder, NASA's solar-powered, remotely piloted aircraft is shown here touching down on Kauai in August 1998 while conducting a series of science flights. These missions were designed to highlight the aircraft's science capabilities while collecting imagery of forest and coastal-zone ecosystems. *NASA Dryden Flight Research Center*

Later in 2001, a Global Hawk conducted a widely publicized, unrefueled, 7,500-mile flight across the Pacific Ocean from North America to Australia. On April 23, after a flight of approximately 22 hours, it touched down autonomously at the Royal Australian Air Force Base at Edinburgh, near Adelaide. Six weeks later, after participating in the joint military exercise designated Tandem Thrust 2001, the RQ-4 returned to the United States, once again flying nonstop across the Pacific.

During the operational evaluation of the Global Hawk, there was clearly a learning curve to be surmounted. In the first two years, there were three aircraft lost to accidents. Two were lost in 1999 due to programming errors, and one crashed at the end of 2001 when the rudder actuator worked loose in flight.

In July 2001, the Air Force chose Beale Air Force Base in northern California as the main operating base for the Global Hawk fleet. The base is remembered as having been the home base to the U.S. Air Force SR-71 Blackbird fleet during the Cold War, and it still serves as home to the U-2 and TR-1 reconnaissance aircraft.

In explaining the choice, General John Jumper, Air Combat Command commander, said, "Collocating Global Hawk with Beale's 9th Reconnaissance Wing and the U-2 mission will ensure Global Hawk transitions smoothly from initial bed-down to full operational capability. It also ensures cultural issues associated with transitioning from manned to unmanned reconnaissance are in the hands of our current high-altitude reconnaissance experts at Beale. They are best suited to complete the transition with the least disruption to the mission."

Later in 2001, Global Hawks were deployed to support U.S. forces in Afghanistan during Operation Enduring Freedom. Beginning with the seventh Global Hawk, which was delivered in February 2003, the mission payloads reflected the experience gained from Operation Enduring Freedom. These include improvements in the new integrated mission management computer system, which controls navigation and the autonomous piloting of the RQ-4.

Onlookers are dwarfed by the 206-foot wingspan of the Centurion flying wing on a hangar ramp at NASA's Dryden Flight Research Center in November 1998. The Centurion went on to demonstrate its flying qualities in late 1998 during three battery-powered flights under control of a ground-based pilot at Dryden. *NASA Dryden Flight Research Center*

The long, curved wing of the Centurion remotely piloted flying wing is clearly visible. This photo was taken during an initial series of low-altitude, battery-powered test flights in late 1998 over California's Mojave Desert. *NASA Dryden Flight Research Center*

Centurion, Helios, and ERAST

Though they are not tactical UAVs, no discussion of very large, very long-range UAVs is possible without mention of the aircraft of NASA's ERAST program, which was ongoing during the 1990s at the same time that the Global Hawk was under development.

The chief focus of the ERAST program was the development of slow, remotely operated aircraft that could perform long-duration scientific missions at altitudes above 60,000 feet. The most extreme mission envisioned by ERAST would reach altitudes of 100,000 feet and include remote sensing for earth sciences studies, hyperspectral imaging for agriculture monitoring, storm tracking, and telecommunications. A parallel effort was the development of lightweight, microminiaturized sensors that could be carried by these aircraft. The tactical applications for such technology are obvious.

The largest UAVs ever built, Centurion and Helios had wingspans greater than a 747 jetliner, and exceeded the 200-foot wingspan of the Boeing Condor UAV that was flight-tested in 1988–1990. Ironically, they were developed by a company that was simultaneously developing some of the tiniest micro air vehicles (MAV) ever built. AeroVironment of Monrovia, California, was founded by Dr. Paul MacCready, a pioneer in solar-powered aircraft. Among his early efforts were the Solar Challenger, Pathfinder, and Pathfinder Plus aircraft, which set an unofficial world altitude record for solar-powered aircraft of 80,201 feet in the summer of 1998.

All of these aircraft were of similar flying-wing design, with each having a larger wingspan than its predecessor. The Pathfinder had a wing spanning 98 feet, the Pathfinder Plus had a wingspan of 121 feet, and the Centurion had a wingspan of 206 feet. In each of these aircraft, solar arrays covered most of the upper wing surface to power the aircraft's electric motors, which numbered 14 on the Centurion and Helios. A lithium battery system provided between two and five hours of backup power.

The Centurion made its first flight on November 10, 1998, but was soon superseded by the huge Helios, which made its debut flight on September 8, 1999, over the NASA Dryden Flight Test Center at Edwards Air Force Base in California. Helios was essentially an enlarged version of the Centurion, with a wingspan of 247 feet. On August 13, 2001, the Helios took off from the U.S. Navy's Pacific Missile Range Facility at Barking Sands on the Hawaiian island of Kauai to set an unofficial world-record altitude of 96,863 feet—with sustained flight above 96,000 feet for more than 40 minutes.

In marked contrast to its extreme-altitude capability, the Helios had an extremely slow cruising speed of about 25 miles per hour. It was also an extremely light aircraft, weighing about 1,600 pounds when fully fitted out with its onboard instrumentation.

The next step in Helios development had been a planned series of long-duration missions. Unfortunately, the program came to an abrupt end on June

Ground crew maneuver AeroVironment's solar-powered Helios prototype flying wing on its ground-support dolly during functional checkouts on April 28, 2001, prior to its first flights under solar power from the U.S. Navy's Pacific missile range facility at Barking Sands on the Hawaiian island of Kauai. *NASA Dryden Flight Research Center*

26, 2003, when the aircraft was lost during a shakedown flight in preparation for a 40-hour mission planned for later in the summer. Helios crashed into the Pacific and sank before it could be recovered. The loss of Helios would not be the end of high-altitude solar aircraft research, and it would be only a matter of time before the lessons learned in the NASA ERAST program found their way into tactical UAV applications.

Micro- and Mini-UAVs

The Micro-UAV or MAV program officially began at DARPA in 1996, but it is clearly a concept with which Reginald Denny would have been familiar in 1936. Simply put, the MAV program is the adaptation and creation of small, RC airplanes for military surveillance tasks. The only thing that would have surprised Mr. Denny would be the way television cameras have been miniaturized. He would have been delighted.

Another term that is often mentioned when MAVs are discussed is the organic air vehicle (OAV). One might suspect that the term *organic* means that they are organically living creatures. In fact, the OAV is defined as a UAV that can be assigned to and used by the smallest operational unit. This would be the U.S. Army squad, which contains a half-dozen soldiers. Parenthetically, up through World War I, the U.S. Army made extensive use of aerial vehicles that *were* organically living creatures. They were called carrier pigeons.

Today, the MAV genre includes a whole archipelago of programs. Because this book is about the evolution of large UAVs into UCAVs, an extended discussion of MAVs is beyond our focus, but they are certainly worth mentioning.

At DARPA, they're often thinking outside the box. The initial thrust of the MAV program was aimed at developing a reconnaissance aircraft smaller than 6 inches in diameter that had a range of 6 miles and an endurance of 20 minutes that could be used by a squad. The idea was—and still is—to give a small unit useful, real-time combat information, especially in difficult terrain, such as in mountains and canyons, heavily forested areas with dense foliage, and even inside buildings!

Among the MAVs that were developed were the Lockheed Martin MicroStar, a battery-operated, propeller-driven winged craft with a teardrop-shaped fuselage. Another MAV was the AeroVironment Black Widow, which was developed in conjunction with UCLA and Cal Tech. Carrier pigeons are slightly larger, but they have a greater range. AeroVironment received DARPA's 1999 Award for outstanding performance by a small business innovation research (SBIR) Contractor for their MAV. DARPA has cited the Black Widow as being potentially valuable to the military as a "fixed-wing squad-level reconnaissance micro air vehicle."

Just 6 inches in diameter, the Black Widow weighs 2 ounces, yet it is capable of speeds up to 43 miles per hour with a battery-powered engine driving a single forward-mounted propeller. For navigation, the Black Widow uses a system of miniature gyroscopes and airflow detectors to measure speed and rate of turn. In turn, this is linked to a GPS unit to confirm its exact location. It can operate for a half-hour with a combat radius of over a mile, returning live color video from its tiny onboard camera. The Black Widow was the smallest, lightest, multifunctional, fully proportional RC aircraft ever flown with a video camera. The 2-gram camera was a precursor to those now found in cell phones.

It seems hard to believe that the Black Widow, which is about the size and shape of a small book, could not only fly, but operate so successfully. An article appearing in the January 9, 1999, issue of the *Economist* magazine in England addressed the issue of how something so nonaerodynamic in appearance could fly, commenting that "The aerodynamics of small things are, however, different from those of larger objects (according to classical theory, for

The Helios flying wing was built by AeroVironment as part of NASA's ERAST program. It is seen here near Kauai on June 7, 2003, during the first flight of a large aircraft to be powered by electric fuel cells. Helios used its solar panels to power its 10 electric motors for takeoff and during daylight portions of its 20-hour shakedown flight. As sunlight diminished, Helios switched to the fuel-cell system to continue flight into the night. *NASA Dryden Flight Research Center*

example, a bumblebee should be unable to fly). That allows for experimentation. Black Widow, designed at AeroVironment, was the first MAV to leave the ground. It looks spookily like a (tiny) flying saucer."

Another 6-inch MAV developed by AeroVironment is the Microbat ornithopter. As the name implies, this vehicle was propelled by flapping its wings in a birdlike fashion. The manned ornithopters of the early twentieth century had failed because their weight could not be supported by flapping wings, but, as has been shown with various model aircraft through the years, smaller-scale ornithopters do work. It was only late in the twentieth century that useful payloads had been miniaturized to the point where ornithopters had the potential for tactical applications.

As for this potential, an article in the July 12, 1998, issue of *Aviation Week* discussed Microbat flight-testing, saying that "Investigators will see if flapping is more efficient than propellers at small scales, whether bird-like aircraft are stealthier and whether there is hope for hummingbird-like vertical flight. AeroVironment has built the 6 inch span, 10 gram device and flown it uncontrolled for 18 seconds and 50 yards. The wings flap at 20 Hz. . . . When the weakened craft lies flopping in the grass (as its batteries ran down), sparrows land next to it. 'They seem to be looking after their fallen comrade,' AeroVironment Project Manager Matt Keennon said."

Though the 6-inch airplanes work, they are susceptible to the wind, and the imagery they transmitted was blurry. At Lockheed's Skunk Works, engineers began to scale up their Micro-Star to try to determine an optimal size—still small, but sufficiently stable to be useful. They determined that a 2-foot wingspan was about the minimum. The McDonnell Douglas (later Boeing) Phantom Works tested a joined-wing aircraft with a 10-foot span under its Project Diamond program in the mid-1990s.

This work continued under the auspices of the force protection airborne surveillance system (FPASS) program. The idea here was a lightweight UAV that could be flown by an operator with no pilot training to provide real-time surveillance beyond the perimeter of a base that was located in hostile territory.

The aircraft selected by the U.S. Air Force to satisfy the FPASS requirement was the Desert Hawk. Developed by the Lockheed Martin Skunk Works, the project was known internally as "Sentry Owl" prior to the contract award from the Air Force, but this working name was never applied to an actual aircraft.

First used operationally during Gulf War II, the Desert Hawk has a wingspan of 52 inches and is less than 3 feet long. Made mostly of mold-injected polypropylene foam, it weighs just 5 pounds and can be operated by a squad or used to monitor a base perimeter. Such airplanes are preprogrammed to fly a particular elliptical flight path. There is no joystick and no pilot. The ellipse is set on the control screen of a laptop and can be changed by the operator.

The Air Force Electronic Systems Center at Hanscom Air Force Base in Massachusetts signed a contract in late February 2002, and Skunk Works delivered the first two six-plane systems 127 days later. By the end of the year, eight systems had been delivered. Each system, including the six Desert

Hawks and their control gear, are packed in a box weighing just over 500 pounds.

Another MAV that evolved into a UAV deployed in Gulf War II was an outgrowth of the Smart warfighting array of reconfigurable modules (SWARM), developed by the Naval Surface Warfare Center. Designed by the ONR to fly in groups—or swarms—the SWARMs were envisioned as low-cost, expendable UAVs that would operate as a cooperative group, replacing individual losses by reconfiguring the group to complete their mission.

With a "plug-and-play" payload capability, the SWARM could be used for ground surveillance, sea search, battle-damage assessment, data-link relay, gunfire control spotting, chemical or biohazard aerial sampling, close-air support, air-defense decoy work, or clandestine "tailing" of surface contacts.

SWARM led to the Silver Fox, a mini-UAV that is built by Advanced Ceramics Research in Tucson, Arizona, from the ONR design. The 20-pound Silver Fox is 5 feet long, with two detachable 4-foot wings, and it looks like one of Reginald Denny's Radioplanes.

Coincidentally, an obscure scientific concept known as "swarm intelligence" had begun to make its way into theoretical planning for twenty-first-century UAV operations. As early as 1992, scientist Eric Bonabeau and biologist Guy Theraulaz had been studying the behavior of social insects such as bees, and they had discovered ways to improve the performance of networks and organizations. By 2003, Bonabeau was working with Bruce McClough in the control automation section of the air vehicle directorate at the U.S. Air Force Research Laboratory,

U.S. Air Force Desert Hawk UAVs were arrayed on the tarmac at the Lockheed Martin Skunk Works facility in Palmdale, California, when photographed in early 2004. *Lockheed Martin—Eric Schulzinger*

where they were studying the application of "swarm tactics" in modern warfare, especially with small and inexpensive UAVs.

In addition to its micro-UAVs, AeroVironment had also produced its FQM-151 Pointer, which is in the same size and weight class as the Silver Fox and Desert Hawk. During the early stages of Operation Enduring Freedom in Afghanistan in the winter of 2001–2002, the U.S. Special Operations Command found itself fighting a close-in war in difficult terrain. This environment was ideal for the Pointer, but, by this time, technology had progressed to the point where AeroVironment could produce an improved variation on the Pointer. Known as the Raven, this vehicle is discussed in the segment on Afghanistan in the following chapter.

A subsequent-generation MAV demonstration aircraft from AeroVironment was the Wasp, which was developed under DARPA's Synthetic Multifunctional Materials program. An RC flying wing with a wingspan of 13 inches, this little system had a total weight, including the battery pack and color video camera, of only 6 ounces. The design replaced separate battery and wing structure components with a multifunctional structure that supplied the electrical energy for propulsion while carrying mechanical and aerodynamic wing loads.

The Wasp used a lithium-ion battery, which produced the highest energy density of any rechargeable battery of its size that was available at the turn of the century. In August 2002, the Wasp set a world endurance record for MAVs with a 107-minute flight.

The ScanEagle UAV made its first autonomous flight on June 19, 2002. Built by the Insitu Group and developed in cooperation with Boeing, the ScanEagle later participated in the U.S. Navy's Giant Shadow experiment at a test site in the Bahamas. *Insitu*

AeroVironment also created the Hornet MAV, which in March 2003 made what was believed to be the world's first successful flight of an unmanned aircraft powered entirely by a hydrogen fuel cell. Developed by Lynntech, the fuel cell was an energy-conversion device in which hydrogen—stored in the form of a dry pellet onboard the aircraft—reacted with oxygen collected from the airflow over the wing to produce electricity. Produced under a DARPA-sponsored research contract to develop innovative propulsion and structural concepts for MAVs, the Hornet made three flights totaling 15 minutes, without the use of batteries, capacitors, or other sources of energy. The Hornet's radio channel link, servos, motor, pumps, and other avionic systems were also all powered by the fuel cell. As with the battery system in the earlier Wasp UAV, the fuel cell also served as a structural component of the 15-inch wing. The total weight of the vehicle was just 6 ounces.

ScanEagle

The ScanEagle is a mini-UAV designed to evaluate the technology for a long-endurance, yet very low-cost vehicle. In February 2002, the project brought together aerospace giant Boeing with the Insitu Group of Bingen, Washington, a company that developed miniature robotic aircraft for both commercial and military use. Having created the first UAV to cross the Atlantic Ocean, Insitu had also originated the Seascan UAV, which was used by the commercial fishing industry for fish spotting. For the ScanEagle program, Insitu built the airframe, and Boeing provided the communications and payload components, as well as systems integration.

Launched by pneumatic catapult, the ScanEagle is 4 feet long, with a wingspan of 10 feet, roughly the same dimensions as the Seascan. It has a top speed of about 80 miles per hour, and is recovered by a sky-hook system involving a line hanging from a 50-foot pole. Designed for missions lasting as long as 40 hours, it was the smallest UAV yet to be equipped with an inertially stabilized gimbaled video camera. As it does for larger aircraft such as the Predator, this system would allow the ScanEagles to track both stationary and moving targets.

The first autonomous flight of the ScanEagle occurred on June 19, 2002, at Boeing's remote test facility near Boardman in eastern Oregon. In this flight, lasting 45 minutes, the ScanEagle flew a pre-programmed course with a maximum altitude of 1,500 feet using GPS.

Eight months later, in February 2003, the little aircraft was transported to the Bahamas to participate in the U.S. Navy's Giant Shadow exercise. In a scenario worthy of Hollywood, the exercise was designed to examine the tactical integration of special operations forces and a stealthy attack submarine with the ScanEagle and an unmanned underwater vehicle. During Giant Shadow, the ScanEagle illustrated its capability to relay real-time data and video.

CHAPTER FOUR

UAVs Go on the Attack

I t is axiomatic that the place of the United States in the world changed dramatically on September 11, 2001. So too, of course, did the role of the U.S. armed forces. In outlining the American response to the terrorist attacks a week later, President George W. Bush promised "a different kind of war."

"It is a different type of battlefield. It is a different type of war," Bush said. "The battles will be fought visibly sometimes, and sometimes we'll never see what may be taking place."

In short, it was a "different kind of war," tailor-made for the capabilities of the generation of UAVs that had been in development since the mid-1990s. When the United States went to war in Afghanistan on October 7, 2001, the U.S. Air Force was operational with the RQ-1 Predator, and the U.S. Navy with the RQ-2 Pioneer. The Air Force RQ-4 Global Hawk was still in flight-testing, but it too would be pressed into service.

"We have to think differently," the president said in a speech two months after the attacks. "The enemy who appeared on September 11 seeks to

avoid our strengths and constantly searches for our weaknesses. So America is required once again to change the way our military thinks and fights."

Though experiments had been undertaken with arming UAVs before, it would be during Operation Enduring Freedom in Afghanistan that the transition would lead from the theoretical to the fully operational. UAVs would help shape the way that the American military "thinks and fights."

Arming the Predator

Though it was named "Predator," the notion of actually arming it to kill prey was secondary to the original surveillance mission. It would take this sudden "different kind of war" to make the Predator into a predator.

On September 6, 2001, less than a week before the United States found itself thrust into that "different kind of war," General John Jumper became chief of staff of the U.S. Air Force. Jumper came to the top job after a year and a half as commander of Air Combat Command, but before that, he had served in the dual role as commander of U.S. Air Forces in Europe (USAFE) and as commander of Allied Air Forces Central Europe (AFCENT). His tenure in these positions—from December 1997 to February 2000— had coincided with Operation Allied Force/Noble

LEFT: Senior Airman Robert Mascorro of the 46th Expeditionary Reconnaissance Squadron directs an MQ-1 Predator at Tallil Air Base in Iraq on January 20, 2004. *Department of Defense—Staff Sergeant Suzanne Jenkins, U.S. Air Force*

As commander of Allied Air Forces Central Europe (AFCENT) in the late 1990s, General John Jumper had firsthand experience with Predators in a combat situation. He became chief of staff of the U.S. Air Force on September 6, 2001, after heading the air combat command for 19 months. *U.S. Air Force*

Anvil in the Balkans. As such, he had direct experience with UAVs in a combat theater.

On his watch, Jumper had seen the Predator go to the Balkans as a surveillance aircraft that had morphed into a targeting tool. The SAR could provide imagery of targets, but it couldn't do anything about taking them out. The Predator could only watch as enemy tanks lumbered toward friendly positions. The laser designator and rangefinder—or "laser ball"—however, could "laze" the tank, or put a laser beam on it so that an F-16 with laser-guided munitions, such as a GBU-24 Paveway III, could find and destroy the target.

Jumper would later describe this transition as "a breakthrough." As he put it, the laser ball "turns the Predator from just a pure surveillance system into something that actually . . . directs weapons on the targets."

The next step, obvious to Jumper and many others, was to actually arm the Predators. However, when he returned to the United States to take over Air Combat Command, Jumper discovered that the

Predators had been turned back into reconnaissance aircraft. When they had been brought home from the Balkans, the laser balls had been removed. The general ordered them reinstalled. He also ordered that the Predators be taken to the next step. General Jumper ordered the Air Force to look into arming Predators.

The immediate problem in arming the small drone was weight. The Predator was never designed to be armed. Its total payload capacity is less than 500 pounds, the weight of the lightest standard "dumb" bomb. Laser-guided GBU-24s weigh four times that. The solution was the laser-guided AGM-114 Hellfire, an air-to-surface, antiarmor missile that had been designed for use aboard Army and Marine Corps attack helicopters. They weigh about 100 pounds each. As Jumper put it, the Hellfire was ideal for what he described as "fleeting, perishable targets that don't require a big warhead that we can just go ahead and take care of."

On February 16, 2001, during tests at Nellis Air Force Base, a Predator successfully fired a Hellfire AGM-114C into a target. The notion of turning the Predator into a *predator* had been realized. No one could imagine that, before the year was out, the Predator would be preying upon live targets in Afghanistan.

War in Afghanistan

On October 7, 2001, the United States launched Operation Enduring Freedom. The Taliban government of Afghanistan was hosting the personnel and infrastructure of the al-Qaeda terrorist gang that had planned and executed the September 11 attacks. Enduring Freedom was aimed at deposing the Taliban, destroying the al-Qaeda infrastructure, and killing or capturing as many al-Qaeda gangsters as possible.

The operation relied heavily on special operations personnel belonging to both the military and to the CIA, supported by U.S. Navy and U.S. Air Force attack aircraft. Because the enemy, especially al-Qaeda, consisted of small bands of personnel that were either on foot or in light vehicles, the Predator was the right weapon for the new kind of battlefield. It was light, quiet, and simple to deploy and operate. It could identify and track targets four or five miles away without being seen. It was also armed.

Though the Predator had come away from the Balkan Wars of the 1990s with a mixed report card, it was high on the list of weapons that the U.S. Central Command (CENTCOM) would deploy in Operation

Against the moody backdrop of darkening clouds, a Predator is on patrol, armed with an AGM-114 Hellfire missile. The tail code identifies it as being based at Nellis Air Force Base, while the insignia on the forward fuselage is that of the 11th Reconnaissance Squadron. *General Atomics Aeronautical Systems*

Enduring Freedom. Like General Jumper of the Air Force, the CENTCOM commander, U.S. Army General Tommy Franks, recognized the Predator's unique capabilities. He included several Predator teams among the first troops he ordered to go overseas. At least one team each had gone to Pakistan and Uzbekistan in September.

Some of the first missions would involve spotting targets for AC-130 gunships. A CENTCOM officer told Richard Newman, writing for *Air Force* magazine, that the Predator allowed the gunships to start hitting the enemy immediately after they arrived in the target area, rather than having to orbit once or twice to get oriented. "The AC-130, when it's teamed with the Predator, pretty much hits what it's going after," he said.

As usually occurs when a new weapon is first sent onto a battlefield, there is a learning curve that sends its creator back to the drawing board. As a surveillance and targeting platform, the Predator was

Personnel from the 11th Reconnaissance Squadron perform preflight checks on an RQ-1 Predator at a forward operating base prior to an Operation Enduring Freedom mission over Afghanistan in November 2001. *U.S. Air Force—Technical Sergeant Scott Reed*

The secret location was undisclosed, but this RQ-4A was certainly based in "Global Hawk Country." The big aircraft is seen here in its personalized hangar at a "forward deployed location," ready to fly its next mission supporting Operation Enduring Freedom. *U.S. Air Force—Staff Sergeant Reynaldo Ramon*

already battle-tested in the Balkans. As an attack platform, it needed some fine-tuning. The Hellfire was designed to be used against tanks and armored vehicles. When it was first used against unarmored, soft targets, the missile sliced through them and penetrated the ground beneath them. The U.S. Army's Redstone Arsenal solved the problem by retrofitting the Hellfires with a fragmentation sleeve.

Other potential problems, such as immediate stress damage to the Predator's fragile composite wing, did not materialize. Nor did carrying the Hellfires degrade the endurance of the Predator. Typically, a Predator flies a 24-hour operational mission, but the extra weight and drag only reduced this by about two hours.

Operated by both the Air Force and the CIA, Hellfire-armed MQ-1s would ultimately prove that it was the ideal weapon to, in General Jumper's words, "take care of a range of targets that we called fleeting and perishable—ones that get away quickly."

Initially, however, the Predators were hamstrung by political considerations in the effort to kill "fleeting and perishable" targets before they could get away. On the first night of the operation, a convoy of vehicles fleeing the city of Kabul reportedly contained the personal SUV of Mullah Omar, the supreme leader of the Taliban. Using high-resolution imaging, an armed Predator is said to have confirmed Omar's presence by reading his license plate.

The CIA controller managing this Predator did not have the authority to order a fire on such a high-value target. The request to take a shot was transmitted to the duty officer at CENTCOM headquarters at MacDill Air Force Base in Florida. It was referred to General Franks, who took the advice of his judge advocate general (JAG) to *not* attack Omar. When Secretary of Defense Donald Rumsfeld learned of this, he was furious and is said to have kicked in a door. He clarified the rules of engagement to ensure that such a thing never happened again.

The opportunity to take out the primary protector of Osama bin Laden had slipped away, but a month later, a Predator played a key role in killing Muhammad Atef, a top al-Qaeda military commander. Shortly after Enduring Freedom had begun, Atef had said, "The calculations of the crusade coalition were very mistaken when it thought it could wage a war on Afghanistan, achieving victory swiftly." However, it was Atef whose miscalculations left his lifeless body amid a pile of broken masonry in

These images of the Taliban's Divisional Regiment Headquarters at Mazar-e-Sharif in Afghanistan were taken by U.S. Air Force Predator drones before and after it was attended to by American strike aircraft on or about October 11, 2001. *Department of Defense*

Pre-strike and post-strike images, such as these October 2001 photographs of Herat Airfield in Afghanistan, were made possible by U.S. Air Force RQ-1 Predators and RQ-4 Global Hawks on the scene during Operation Enduring Freedom. *Department of Defense*

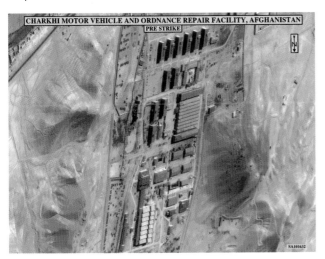

The angle of these photos of the Taliban's Charkhi motor vehicle and ordnance repair facility in Afghanistan suggests that they were taken by an RQ-1 Predator flying relatively low. These images were officially released on October 15, 2001. *Department of Defense*

A U.S. Navy SEAL scans the rugged landscape of eastern Afghanistan during a sensitive site exploitation (SSE) mission on February 12, 2002, during Operation Enduring Freedom. This is the type of terrain in which ground operations are greatly aided by the use of reconnaissance UAVs. *U.S. Navy—Photographer's Mate 1st Class Tim Turner*

gangsters Qaed Senyan Al-Harthi and Kamal Derwish in Yemen on November 4, 2002.

After Afghanistan and Yemen, the Predator had emerged as one of the unexpected rising stars in the U.S. arsenal—and a poster child for the effectiveness of *armed* UAVs. In a Pentagon briefing given on the last day of October 2001, a senior defense official—who wished only to be identified as such—commented that the Predator had been "deployed continuously since 1996 and all the theater commanders are begging for more Predators. . . .[F]or what it does do, it does a great job."

The Global Hawk also joined the action in the skies over Afghanistan in early November 2001. With its synthetic SAR, the huge RQ-4 offered an all-weather surveillance capability that was much needed because of the winter storms and constant cloud cover. It also offered the unprecedented ability to remain over a battlefield for more than 24 hours, providing a continuous stream of data.

The RQ-4's operational debut had come much sooner than expected. As had been the case with the E-8 J-STARS aircraft in 1991 during Gulf War I, the RQ-4 was still being flight-tested, but commanders in the field needed its capabilities—so it went to war. The Global Hawk would be assigned to the 12th Expeditionary Reconnaissance Squadron (a

Kabul. The Taliban itself confirmed his demise on November 17.

A Predator had been only one of the players in the Atef strike, but a year later, the Predator firmly staked out its place in the history of warfare. As discussed in the prologue, it would be a lone Predator—and that Predator alone—that took out al-Qaeda

Airman 1st Class John Mosher, an avionics specialist with the 11th Expeditionary Reconnaissance Squadron, removes the wheel chocks from an RQ-1B Predator prior to an Operation Enduring Freedom mission in Afghanistan during 2002. *U.S. Air Force—Technical Sergeant Joe Springfield*

Airman 1st Class John D. Clark from the 15th Reconnaissance Squadron, based at Nellis Air Force Base, performs maintenance on a Predator UAV after its return from a reconnaissance flight over Afghanistan in February 2002. *U.S. Marine Corps—Chief Warrant Officer 2nd Class William Crow*

An MQ-9A Predator B "Hunter-Killer" UAV is shown in flight over a desert landscape. First flown in 2001, the Predator B is a third larger than its older sibling and capable of more than three times the payload of the MQ-1. *General Atomics Aeronautical Systems*

component of the 9th Reconnaissance Wing at Beale Air Force Base), which was based at an undisclosed forward operating location in southwest Asia close to Afghanistan.

The Global Hawk's baptism of fire was marred by a crash that took place on December 30, 2001, about 80 miles from its operating base. An accident investigation would later determine that the RQ-4 was not shot down. Rather, the accident was the result of the structural failure of the right V-tail due to massive delamination of the main spar, precipitated by a control-rod failure. The latter happened when the rod came in contact with an improperly installed actuator nut plate bolt. Simple screwups can have massive ramifications.

By December 2001, the Taliban had largely been defeated in most of Afghanistan. Major Taliban and al-Qaeda bases were in American hands, and the surviving enemy had been squeezed into the rugged and mountainous Tora Bora region in the southeast, near Afghanistan's border with Pakistan.

In a December 17 Pentagon briefing, Rear Admiral John Stufflebeem, a spokesman for the Joint Chiefs of Staff, said that catching the enemy "on the run" in the mountains and caves around Tora Bora was like "searching for fleas on a dog. . . . If you see one, you don't know how many others are getting away. Every cave that is entered is being treated as a hostile environment. While the fierce fighting we've seen up to a few hours ago may have subsided a little bit, it now becomes the more difficult and the slow process of confirming who is left to fight."

Air power pounded the cave complexes where the enemy was hiding, but on the ground, the going was not easy. American special operations troops were not large in number, and when it came to "boots on the ground," the Americans had to rely mainly on the not-always-reliable Afghan irregulars of the Eastern Alliance. Many al-Qaeda and Taliban were being killed or captured, but others—including terrorist boss Osama bin Laden and Khalid Sheikh Mohammed, the mastermind of the September 11 attacks—managed to get away. The latter would be nabbed in Pakistan 14 months later.

The extent of the role played by the Predators in the Tora Bora battles remains largely classified, but it is known that they were used extensively. They were seen at forward operating locations wearing numerous "mission marks," implying numerous completed sorties.

These missions continued. In southeastern Afghanistan, on February 4, 2002, a CIA-controlled Predator fired a Hellfire missile at a group of men suspected of being senior al-Qaeda leaders—possibly including bin Laden. However, forensic evidence subsequently recovered from the site determined that bin Laden was not among those killed.

The Honeywell TPE 331-10T turboprop of an MQ-9A Predator B winds up for takeoff. In addition to being larger than the Predator, the Predator B is distinguished from the Predator by its distinctly different tail configuration. *General Atomics Aeronautical Systems*

"There are no initial indications that these were innocent locals," Admiral Stufflebeem said at a subsequent Pentagon briefing in response to media speculation. "I base that on the facts that this [forensic] team, in addition to just looking at the site where the strike occurred, also did some exploration in the surrounding area to include some caves, a nearby village, and talked to locals." Among the items found at the site were documents in English, missile fins, AK-47 ammunition pouches, and .50-caliber ammunition.

While the Predator and Global Hawk may have received the most attention for UAV operations in Afghanistan, others were also involved. These included compact, "back-packable" mini-UAVs such as the Lockheed Martin Desert Hawk and AeroVironment's Pointer and Raven. The AeroVironment FQM-151 Pointer had been used in Gulf War I and was present in Afghanistan in the winter

The General Atomics Altair is a high-altitude version of the Predator B, which was specifically designed as an unmanned platform for both scientific and commercial research missions that require endurance and increased payload capacity. *General Atomics Aeronautical Systems*

Armed with AGM-114 Hellfires, an MQ-1 Predator is cleared for takeoff on an Operation Enduring Freedom mission over Afghanistan in March 2003. *U.S. Air Force—Staff Sargent Jeremy Lock*

of 2001–2002, when the U.S. Special Operations Command found itself fighting the kind of war where a back-packable UAV could be a tremendous asset. The close-in war in difficult terrain was ideal for a UAV such as the FQM-151, but, by this time, technology had progressed to the point where AeroVironment could produce an improved variation on the Pointer.

During the first year of Operation Enduring Freedom, the Special Operations Command also ordered more than 80 Raven mini-UAVs. Based on the Pointer, the new, scaled-down Raven vehicle had a wingspan of 4 feet 3 inches, compared to the Pointer's 9-foot span. When folded down and packed for transport, it weighs just 8.5 pounds. Like the Pointer, the Raven is easy to operate for a "pilot" with minimal training. Another advantage that the mini-UAVs have demonstrated is the way that their endurance can be extended by riding thermal air currents, just like a bird of prey.

Though they are outside the scope of this book, it is worth mentioning that the U.S. Army deployed unmanned ground vehicles (UGV) to Afghanistan. The 40-pound, tracked Packbots were used to search the caves and tunnel complexes. Packbots would also be deployed to Iraq during Gulf War II in 2003, along with the similar, 50-pound Matilda UGVs. They are operated remotely through a television link and are powered by electric motors.

Lessons had been learned from the operational UAV deployments to the Balkans, and so too were lessons derived from the Afghanistan experience that would help refine the use of UAVs in combat. One of the most important was what the Defense Department called "interoperability." This was the ability of the various services to communicate with one another's UAVs in combat situations. One of the Navy-led joint projects was the Tactical Control System. This gave commanders the ability to command and control UAVs belonging to other services, and to disseminate information across a wide number of command and control nodes.

The office of the secretary of defense had also authorized a joint test and evaluation of tactics, techniques, and procedures involving tactical UAVs and time-critical operations. This was a joint operation involving the Army, Air Force, Navy, and the Marine Corps.

As has been true throughout the history of weapons development, practical experience always shapes the evolution of military technology. In a Pentagon briefing on August 2, 2002, Victoria Clarke, the assistant secretary of defense for public affairs, summed it up by saying that, in the war on terrorism, American forces were "always looking for ways to be more adaptive, to be more flexible, to be faster, to be more lethal, to go after what is a very unconventional enemy."

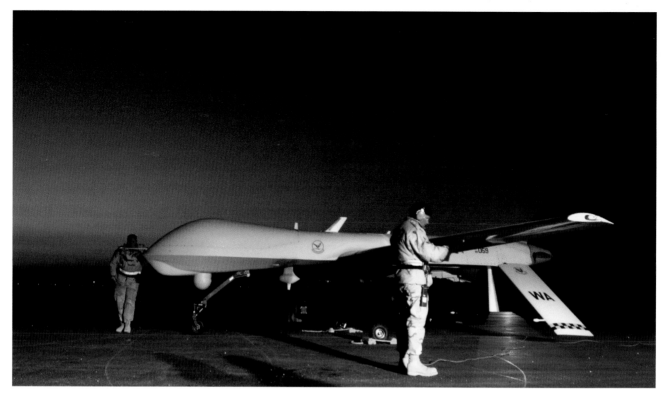

Maintenace workers perform last-minute preflight checks on an RQ-1 Predator at a forward-deployed location before an Operation Iraqi Freedom misssion in March 2003. *U.S. Air Force—Staff Sargent Jeremy Lock*

Even the president of the United States was pleased with the way that the Predator performed during Enduring Freedom. In a speech at the Citadel in Charleston, South Carolina, on December 11, George W. Bush said, "These past two months have shown that innovative doctrine and high-tech weaponry can shape and then dominate an unconventional conflict. . . . Our commanders are gaining a real-time picture of the entire battlefield, and are able to get targeting information from sensor to shooter almost instantly. . . . Before the war, the Predator had skeptics because it did not fit the old ways. Now it is clear the military does not have enough unmanned vehicles."

Predator B and Altair

A year before combat in the unexpected war in Afghanistan turned the Predator into a pivotal weapons system, General Atomics had been working on the much larger Predator B multimission hunter-killer aircraft, which would enter service with the U.S. Air Force under the designation MQ-9A. Developed in 2000, with a first flight in February 2001, the Predator B is 36 feet long, with a wingspan of 66 feet. Powered by a Honeywell TPE 331-10T turboprop engine, it has a cruising speed of 250 miles per hour,

an operational altitude of 50,000 feet, and an endurance in excess of 30 hours. The aircraft weighs 10,000 pounds, with an internal payload of 800 pounds and an external payload of 3,000 pounds, substantially more than the MQ-1 Predator.

While the MQ-1 is typically armed with the AGM-114 Hellfire missile, the MQ-9 can carry the AGM-65 Maverick, a much more potent air-to-ground weapon designed for such heavy-duty tasks as busting tanks. Ironically, it had been an early version of the Maverick that had been test-fired from a Firebee UAV three decades before Operation Enduring Freedom.

In June 2003, General Atomics Aeronautical Systems unveiled the Altair aircraft, the long-range variant of the Predator B, in a debut flight from the company's El Mirage flight operations facility in California. Altair was developed in conjunction with NASA to conduct high-altitude scientific research. In February 2004, General Atomics announced a contract with the Canadian Armed Forces to deploy the Altair in support of the Atlantic Littoral Intelligence, Surveillance, Reconnaissance Experiment (ALIX). This exercise involved the use of a multimode maritime radar, as well as an electro-optical, infrared camera for surveillance off the east coast of Canada.

Senior Airman Joseph Gollhofer, a 46th Expeditionary Reconnaissance Squadron crew chief, cleans the small lens that the ground-bound pilots will use to fly this MQ-1 Predator on its next Operation Iraqi Freedom mission. Pilots describe the view as like "seeing through a straw." *U.S. Air Force—Technical Sergeant Dan Neely*

Staff Sergeant James Barr, a maintenance member of the 46th Expeditionary Reconnaissance Squadron, connects an aircraft starter cart to an RQ-1 Predator to start the engine for an Operation Iraqi Freedom mission. *U.S. Air Force— Technical Sergeant Dan Neely*

War in Iraq

Even as the United States was pursuing the global war on terrorism that began in 2001, it made the decision to pursue a parallel effort to remove the threat of the Baathist regime of Saddam Hussein in Iraq. Officially designated as Operation Iraqi Freedom, this effort began on March 19, 2003. The first phase, involving the defeat of Saddam's conventional surface forces and the military occupation of Iraq, was declared complete by President Bush on the first of May.

Gulf War II, as the conflict came to be called, was the first large-scale surface war in history in which UAV deployment was an integral part of planning and execution of operations. UAVs were written into the plan from the beginning, and, from the first moment of the action, they demonstrated that they were not simply a vital weapons system, but virtually indispensable.

The UAVs used in the war included the huge RQ-4 Global Hawk loitering high over the battle-field and the RQ-1/MQ-1 Predators, which had already proven themselves as important tactical vehicles in Afghanistan. The Air Force had Predators in the vicinity of Baghdad from the beginning of the war, and Global Hawks over Baghdad, operating in a continuous orbit running as far north as Kirkuk and Urbil.

Indeed, UAVs had been in action over Iraq even before March 19 as part of Operations Northern Watch and Southern Watch, the combat air patrols over the "no-fly" zones in Iraq that had been ongoing since the end of Gulf War I in 1991. Indeed, when a Predator was shot down over southern Iraq on December 23, 2002, it was widely covered in the world media and seen by some as the "first shot" of an impending Gulf War II. Air Force General Richard Myers, the chairman of the Joint Chiefs of Staff, noted Iraq had been trying to shoot down coalition aircraft for several years, and called it "a lucky shot."

He added that this had not been the first time that Iraqi gunners had shot down a Predator. A Defense Department spokesman confirmed that as many as three Predators had been shot down by antiaircraft fire during 2001 in the no-fly zones in northern and southern Iraq. To put this incident into the context of this book, the losses of the Predators are a clear indication of operations in dangerous areas where the loss of a human pilot would not have been risked. The little robots had given their lives to get the pictures.

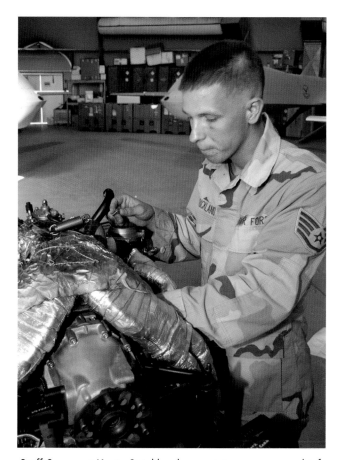

Senior Airman Jason Biselx, a 46th Expeditionary Reconnaissance Squadron crew chief, checks a brake assembly on one of his unit's MQ-1 Predators during a preflight inspection. Said Biselx, "During a one-week period early in Operation Iraqi Freedom, we had major engine overhauls every night." *U.S. Air Force—Technical Sergeant Dan Neely*

Staff Sergeant Kevin Strickland, a maintenance crew chief with the 46th Expeditionary Reconnaissance Squadron, works on an RQ-1 Predator's Rotax 914 engine at a forward-deployed location during Operation Iraqi Freedom. His task was part of a time-phased engine overhaul procedure. *U.S. Air Force—Technical Sergeant Dan Neely*

One such incident soon after the start of Gulf War II provided the world with almost comical television footage. Several Predators were sent in low over Baghdad to ascertain the levels of enemy air defenses. To the surprise of Air Force commanders, most survived this decoy mission. One Predator, however, went down in the Tigris River in the heart of Baghdad. Iraqi television crews were dispatched to film a frantic search for the pilot of the downed aircraft. Dozens of uniformed and civilian men took part in the search, but the pilot was never found. He was 200 miles away in his control station.

The use of UAVs as reconnaissance platforms in Iraq proceeded seamlessly before and after March 19, but the first use of a Predator in an offensive combat role occurred three days into the war. On March 22, a U.S. Air Force MQ-1 Predator remotely piloted by Major Mark Lilly found and destroyed an

Iraqi ZSU-23-4 mobile, radar-guided antiaircraft artillery gun outside the town of al-Amarah using a single AGM-114K Hellfire II missile. In just over two years, such a capability had gone from an untested theory through a tentative baptism of fire in Afghanistan to being an accepted part of routine battlefield operations in a conventional war.

During the early stages of Gulf War II, the principal operating base for Predators and other tactical UAVs would be Ali al Salem Air Base, just west of Kuwait City. Predators also operated from bases in Jordan, but as the war progressed, UAV operations were relocated to forward operating bases inside Iraq. Organizationally, Predators of the 11th Reconnaissance Squadron were assigned to the 386th Air Expeditionary Wing. Predators were also operated by the 46th Expeditionary Reconnaissance Squadron, which eventually was based at Tallil Air Base inside Iraq.

Day-to-day operations involved the Predators flying missions of about 20 hours. They were operated remotely by a pilot and sensor operator, who worked from a satellite-linked ground-control station. Continuous real-time surveillance of the battlefield was passed along to the theater air-component commander. The Predator teams also included crew chiefs and specialists in avionics, ground equipment, communications, satellite communications, munitions, and supply.

As the surface forces of the U.S. Army's 3rd Infantry Division were attacking north toward Baghdad, Predators were providing ground commanders with real-time information about enemy forces that lay ahead. Said Air Force Captain Traz Trzaskoma, a Predator pilot, in an interview with *Air Force Print News*, "We've been watching for where the bad guys hide, move or want to hide, and if we're carrying Hellfire missiles, we can take care of a target ourselves."

With their LLTV and real-time video stream, Predators were also an invaluable resource for special forces teams operating behind enemy lines. "A special forces team was going into an area, and at the last minute we [told them] their landing zone wasn't the best," Trzaskoma said. "We helped change the mission at the last second. Then we helped them find a better place to land."

Among their work in support of special operations, Predators were involved in the well-documented rescue of Private Jessica Lynch. In another incident, a Predator flown by Major John Breeden was providing surveillance for U.S. Marines and British commandos tasked with the capture of the oil fields near the al-Faw Peninsula in southern Iraq. He spotted a force of approximately 200 enemy troops preparing an ambush and was able to call in a U.S. Air Force AC-130 Specter gunship to hose down the Iraqi position with high-caliber automatic weapons fire.

Commanders on the ground came to rely heavily on the utility of the Predators as the ground war extended across Iraq and U.S. forces met with more-concentrated enemy resistance. This led to a remarkably high operational demand for the services of a relatively small fleet of RQ-1/MQ-1 aircraft. Predators were in service 24 hours a day. "With the enormous amount of hours we fly, our down time is almost nonexistent," said Sergeant Jeffery Duckett, a Predator maintenance superintendent. "What that means is that everyone has to perform top-notch maintenance every day to sustain our wartime taskings. Take away any one of these components, and our mission effectiveness degrades significantly."

Airman Jason Biselx, a Predator crew chief, told *Air Force Print News* that "The main challenge of 24-hour ops with long-endurance missions is the

An RQ-2 Pioneer kicks up dust as it comes in for a landing on the dirt airstrip at Camp Babylon near the Euphrates River in Iraq on June 13, 2003. *Army Staff Sergeant David Bennett*

The U.S. Air Force RQ-4 Global Hawks flew high above the Operation Iraqi Freedom battlefield from bases in Qatar and elsewhere. They operated in conjunction with manned U-2 aircraft and other secret, high-altitude UAVs whose presence was not officially acknowledged during Gulf War II. *Northrop Grumman Media Relations*

Senior Airman Brady Martindale (left) and First Lieutenant Andrew Hackleman inspect the main landing gear of an MQ-1 Predator after a mission over Iraq on July 21, 2003. Martindale was an avionics specialist, and Hackleman a maintenance officer with the 332nd Air Expeditionary Wing at Tallil Air Base in Iraq. *U.S. Air Force—Second Lieutenant Gerardo Gonzalez*

amount of periodic and phased maintenance needed. Time-change items come up faster, phases arrive quicker, and major engine overhauls start to really stack up. During a one-week period early in Operation Iraqi Freedom, we had major engine overhauls every night. Another key challenge is fine tuning a small, dual-carbureted engine for high-altitude, long-endurance flight."

While the Predators garnered much of the media attention devoted to UAVs during Gulf War II, the RQ-4 Global Hawks provided much of the theater-wide strategic reconnaissance upon which the senior planners at CENTCOM based their day-to-day war plans. Indeed, when offensive operations practically ground to a halt during the sandstorms that raged from March 24 to 27, Global Hawks casually observed enemy troop movements, using their SAR to look through the swirling sand as though it was not there. A Global Hawk working in cooperation with an E-8 J-STARS aircraft is credited with providing tactical commanders with the data that resulted in the virtual obliteration of the Iraqi Medina armored division.

The Global Hawks operated with much the same payload package as the manned U-2s, but, while the U-2 pilots had to land in order to sleep, RQ-4 pilots simply turned the controls over to another pilot while the aircraft itself remained aloft on its 24- to 40-hour mission. When the big aircraft landed at bases such as in Qatar, the turnaround time for the next mission was relatively short. According to Tim Beard of Northrop Grumman, this turnaround time between flights was as little as eight hours.

One of the interesting results of the Global Hawk's success in Gulf War II was attracting the German government as a potential customer. Germany, which had opted out of the U.S.-led effort to dispose of Saddam Hussein, had watched the war from the sidelines. Impressed by the big UAV, Germany began to consider its potential use in long-range maritime patrol missions. A few months after the war, Germany's Luftwaffe invited a Global Hawk team to visit their base at Nordholz for a multimission demonstration. A footnote to this deployment was that for the first time, a very large UAV operated within the air traffic control system that governs Europe's highly congested air space. Based on the German expression of interest, Northrop Grumman would propose working with the European Aeronautic Defense and Space Company (EADS), to create a specially modified variation on the RQ-4 that would be known as EuroHawk.

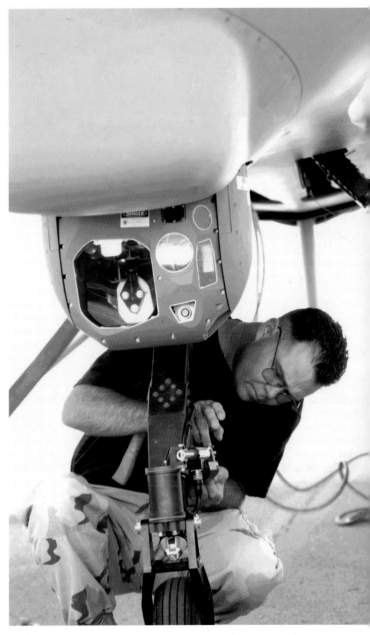

Technical Sergeant Thomas McGuire inspects the nose landing gear of an MQ-1 Predator UAV after a mission over Iraq on July 21, 2003. McGuire was a production superintendent deployed with the 332nd Air Expeditionary Wing to Tallil Air Base. *U.S. Air Force—Second Lieutenant Gerardo Gonzalez*

Another potential user of the Global Hawk that emerged after it had proven itself in Gulf War II was the Defense Department's own National Geospatial Intelligence Agency (formerly the National Imagery and Mapping Agency). Toward the end of 2003 the agency—which had already ordered two MQ-9 Predator B aircraft—floated the idea that it wanted to "borrow" two Air Force RQ-4s to use for evaluating various payloads, including bomb-detection devices.

LEFT: At Tallil Air Base in Iraq, Staff Sergeant Joseph Vialpando (left) and Staff Sergeant Michael Roth prepare a Desert Hawk aircraft for flight in October 2003. The lightweight drone was part of the force protection airborne surveillance system (FPASS) used here to look over the horizon for terrorist activities. Vialpando and Roth were part of the 332nd Expeditionary Security Forces Squadron. *U.S. Air Force—Master Sergeant Don Perrien*

RIGHT: A Desert Hawk launches as Senior Airman David Tillery stands fast. Tillery was assigned to the 332nd Expeditionary Security Forces Squadron, which deployed from Shaw Air Force Base in South Carolina to Balad Air Base in Iraq. *U.S. Air Force—Staff Sergeant A. C. Eggman*

While the U.S. Air Force and the U.S. Army relied on the Predator for real-time battlefield surveillance, the Marine Corps operated their own fleet of RQ-2 Pioneer UAVs. Two Marine UAV Squadrons, VMU-1 and VMU-2, supported the Marines' drive toward Baghdad through the river valleys of eastern Iraq.

The Pioneers and their crews quickly demonstrated the sort of battlefield flexibility that commanders had always hoped for when deploying small UAVs such as the RQ-2. From their original base at Camp Coyote in Kuwait, the Pioneer teams followed the troops on the road to Baghdad. "We worked out of the sides of roads," said Major John Pryce, the operations officer for VMU-2. Eventually, VMU-2 was able to consolidate its operations deep inside Iraq at al-Kut.

As the tanks and troops of the 1st Marine Division neared the Iraqi capital, the Pioneers scouted the road ahead, spotting numerous artillery pieces that could then be taken out with the Marines' own guns. Near Suwarah, a Pioneer picked out a Scud medium-range ballistic missile. In an interview with *Marine Corps News*, Lieutenant Colonel Robert Rice, commander of VMU-2, said, "Because of the Pioneers and their operators, the Iraqi military didn't get the chance to use these weapons against advancing coalition troops."

From al-Kut, VMU-2 moved north to a base at al-Hillah on the banks of the Euphrates River near Baghdad, as the conflict transitioned from a

LEFT: Senior Airman David Tillery (left) and Technical Sergeant Lloyd Joyner of the 332nd Expeditionary Security Forces Squadron look over their Desert Hawk drone after a mission at Balad Air Base in Iraq. The 7-pound UAV allowed security forces to see beyond the base's perimeters and provide accurate, real-time visual assessments of detected threats. *U.S. Air Force—Staff Sergeant A. C. Eggman*

An RQ-1 Predator UAV taxis to the runway at Balad Air Base in Iraq to begin a mission in January 2004. Long after the "major combat" phase of Operation Iraqi Freedom had ended, Predators and other UAVs remained a vital part of U.S. operations. *U.S. Air Force—Staff Sergeant C. E. Lewis*

conventional battlefield conflict to a hunt for Baathist and al-Qaeda irregulars. This base, located near the main Marine base at Camp Babylon, had a 960-foot-long dirt landing strip that some Marines compared with Henderson Field, the unpaved landing strip on Guadalcanal that was used by Marine Corps pilots of the "Cactus Air Force" during 1942 and 1943.

One of the missions assigned to VMU-2 was target location and battle-damage assessment for Marine Corps pilots flying manned AV-8B Harrier attack aircraft. The Pioneers flew at an altitude of 10,000 feet and provided target imagery and position directly to the Harrier pilots, who could then go in for the attack. Afterward, the UAV gathered the battle-damage results.

While the Marines operated the RQ-2 Pioneer in Iraq, the U.S. Army used the similar, twin-boomed RQ-5 Hunter and its newer brother, the RQ-7 Shadow, in a tactical reconnaissance role. During the early days of the war, the Army UAVs shared an operational base with the Air Force Predators at Camp New Jersey in Kuwait.

The Marines also used the diminutive Dragon Eye Micro-UAV. Manufactured by AeroVironment, the Dragon Eye can be likened to a very sophisticated RC model. Weighing less than 6 pounds, it is carried in a backpack and is easily operated by infantrymen. It has a range of just a few miles, but its two-hour endurance is quite useful for troops who want to have a good look over the next hill.

The Dragon Eye had notable success operating at night, underscoring the oft-repeated dictum that U.S. troops "own" the nocturnal battlefield. The U.S. Navy version of the Dragon Eye has been nicknamed "Sea All," a barely forgivable pun.

The Navy also deployed the small Silver Fox tactical UAV that was then in the development stage. Launched from a catapult aboard a ship, the 20-pound Silver Fox has an endurance of five hours. The Navy hopes to quadruple this endurance capability, but it had not developed the Silver Fox that far by the time of Gulf War II.

As the new-technology UAVs grabbed a great deal of the media attention during Gulf War II, older drones were also in action. In February 2003, the Department of Defense gave Northrop Grumman a quick-reaction request to modify both BQM-34 Firebee and BQM-74 Chukar drones for use as chaff-dispensing pathfinders for cruise missiles and strike aircraft. The company reportedly was able to have five Firebees ready in just 17 days.

On the first night of the war, a malfunction grounded the single DC-130 aircraft that remained in the Department of Defense inventory, so two Firebees were ground launched. On the second night, the DC-130 was able to go to work, and the remaining Firebee missions could now be air launched. The Pentagon was reported to have been so pleased with the performance of the Firebee and Chukar that new production of the Firebee was considered, and the latest-version Chukar, the BQM-74F, was fast-tracked.

As the Americans were pleased with their UAVs, so too were the British army with their homegrown Phoenix UAV. A project dating back to the 1980s, the Phoenix had not entered service until 1999 and had encountered many teething troubles during its initial deployment to the Balkans. In Iraq, 80 Phoenixes were used for a variety of roles, including battle-damage assessment and artillery spotting. According to Royal Army Colonel Kevin Harvey, a third of British artillery rounds fired during Gulf War II were directed by a Phoenix.

Though it did not officially acknowledge the fact during Gulf War II, the U.S. Air Force also deployed the highly classified successor to the RQ-3 DarkStar to the skies high over Iraq. Reportedly, its existence was not known until Air Force reconnaissance pilots flying U-2s reported an unidentified aircraft flying near them at extremely high altitudes. A product of Lockheed Martin's Skunk Works, this mysterious new aircraft was reportedly still in the experimental stage, but it had reached a point in its flight-test program where flying it in combat was beneficial for both project evaluation as well as for the tactical value that it might provide for troops involved in the battle. Known unofficially as the "Son of Dark-Star," this mystery ship is said to be a stealth aircraft—unlike either the Global Hawk UAV or the manned U-2.

As the "major combat" phase came to an end in Iraq, U.S. forces found themselves still at war—but a different kind of war. This new phase in the war in Iraq included guerilla-type attacks on American bases and facilities, as well as ground-launched missile attacks against American aircraft landing or taking off. It was the type of situation that had been foreseen a few years earlier when the U.S. Air Force had decided to develop a UAV FPASS. This program had resulted in the Lockheed Martin Desert Hawk UAV, which had been deployed to the theater even before Operation Iraqi Freedom got under way in March.

Like the Marine Corps Dragon Eye, the Air Force Desert Hawk is a radio-controlled, backpack-portable UAV that has an endurance of an hour or so, and a range of several miles. In Iraq, the Desert Hawk would be in operation with a number of units, including the 72nd, 332nd, and 380th Expeditionary Security Forces Squadrons. Easy to use and launched with a bungee cord, the Desert Hawks could provide real-time digital imagery to security forces on the ground.

The Desert Hawk launch sequence is quite simple and very low tech. Launch crews can be set up for a launch in about 10 minutes. The operators attach a bungee cord to the vehicle, which is held in place by one person while another stretches the cord to its maximum extension of about 300 feet. The operator releases the Desert Hawk, which slides forward and starts climbing.

"Desert Hawk allows us to interdict our adversaries before they are able to threaten [airmen] and resources," said Major Glen Christensen, commander of the 332nd Expeditionary Security Forces Squadron. "With this equipment, we can achieve the desired . . . base defense."

"It's a force multiplier," said Master Sergeant Randy Morningstar in an Air Force news service interview. "If you see something [of interest] when it's up in the air, you can send a command to the [UAV] and have it do a tight orbit over [the] top of it so the camera is centered over whatever you see. . . . [Desert Hawk will] go and do whatever you tell it to."

The Desert Hawk's cameras record every flight digitally even as real-time images are streamed to the operator's laptop computer that is as much as three miles away. "It's very, very small and very hard to see," said Staff Sergeant Elizabeth Staub, another Desert Hawk operator. "It's only 52 inches wide and 32 inches long. It's a little bitty thing . . . made out of what they call durable foam. Think Tupperware."

"The manual describes the plane as a state-of-the-art composite material, but it's actually got a lot more in common with a Styrofoam cup than anything else," said Staff Sergeant Michael Roth, the Desert Hawk program manager for the 332nd Expeditionary Security Forces Squadron. "It's pretty tough, but we can glue it back together if it breaks."

As early as the first week of April 2003, General Michael Moseley, the commander of CENTCOM Air Forces, had summarized the value of UAVs, not just in Gulf War II, but in the future of warfare: "They're amazing systems and they provide a capability and a set of options for the air commander, for the commander in chief and the other component commanders that's just outstanding. We're at a threshold of something very, very exciting and very, very new with unmanned aerial vehicles, whether they are unmanned combat aerial vehicles or . . . reconnaissance UAVs." The role of UAVs, as well of UCAVs, on the battlefields of the twenty-first century was assured.

CHAPTER FIVE

The Unmanned
Combat Aerial Vehicle

In the summer of 2001, a few months before the September 11 attacks and before General John Jumper became chief of staff of the U.S. Air Force, he told John Tirpik of *Air Force Magazine*, "I don't think there's any doubt that . . . UCAVs [unmanned combat aerial vehicles] will come, and we will work with the concept of operations to include them." General Jumper's comments would prove to be prophetic.

The November 4, 2002, strike in Yemen was, for the UCAV concept, the sort of turning point that historians and chronology compilers like. It was a clear, definable point in time when people generally sat up and took notice. The Predator actions in Iraq during the spring of 2003 added to the folklore and added credibility to the concept.

Released in March 2003, the U.S. Department of Defense report entitled *Unmanned Aerial Vehicles Roadmap* articulated an integrated policy for UAVs and UCAVs, which outlined the development of

LEFT: Released at the turn of the century, this photo illustration of the Boeing Phantom Works X-45B is an excellent view of unmanned combat aerial vehicles (UCAVs) in tactical war paint. At the time, the notion of unmanned aircraft flying offensive combat missions was still an unorthodox concept that had yet to be fully embraced by traditional strategists. *Boeing Phantom Works*

such aircraft for the quarter century ending in 2027. The executive summary of the document noted that "The overarching goal of this roadmap, in concert with the Defense Planning Guidance (DPG), is to define clear direction to the Services and Departments for a logical, systematic migration of mission capabilities to a new class of military tools. The goal is to address the most urgent mission needs that are supported both technologically and operationally by various UAV systems."

The report noted that "Some missions can be supported by the current state of the art in unmanned technology," but that there were "other mission areas . . . in desperate need of additional capability and [which] present high risk to aircraft crews. These mission areas, highlighted in this roadmap, will receive significant near-term effort by the Department." These mission areas were offensive combat operations, and the roadmap went on to clearly underscore the need to assign resources to meet the twenty-first-century need for UCAVs.

However, the reality of history is that it is filled with precursor moments that go unnoticed. It can be said that the UCAV was born in 1971, when the Air Force first hung a Maverick on a Firebee, and the 2003 *Roadmap* did mention the Vietnam-era UAVs in passing. Of course, the armed Firebee

ABOVE: This dramatic photo shows the Boeing X-45A prototype aircraft undergoing an engine checkout during the spring of 2001 at the Dryden Flight Research Center at Edwards Air Force Base. *DARPA*

This high-angle view shows the assembly of the first X-45A prototype aircraft at the Phantom Works in St. Louis during December 1999. The rollout was nine months away. *DARPA*

Parked on the Dryden Flight Research Center tarmac with Rogers Dry Lake in the background, the first Boeing X-45A prototype aircraft undergoes electromagnetic interference (EMI) tests during the spring of 2001. *DARPA*

never saw action, and despite some field experiments, such as arming a SkyEye in Central America during the 1980s, the UCAV concept languished at the fringes of the defense establishment until the mid-1990s. At the same time that the very sophisticated RQ-3 DarkStar and RQ-4 Global Hawk UAVs were in development, the Defense Department decided to get serious about UCAVs.

Air Force Colonel Mike Francis, the director of architecture and integration at the Defense Airborne Reconnaissance Office, was certainly thinking outside the box in which many of his predecessors had operated. In 1997, he told David Fulghum of *Aviation Week* that his agency was taking a keen interest in armed drones. Said Francis, "We know where manned aircraft are going. For example, if everybody is flying the same [manned] aircraft, the imbalance offered by the introduction of an [unmanned] aircraft that can turn at 20G" could give the advantage to the latter.

Francis then asked rhetorically, "Why put the pilot in a volume and weight constrained space"

if you don't have to? He went so far as to say that in the twenty-first century, UCAVs "could redefine the aircraft carrier as an aircraft that carries other aircraft."

Though such a thought might not have leaped so easily to the mind of a navy man, the chief of naval operations had also commissioned a study of UCAVs in 1997. Again, the future use of UCAVs was embraced. In a prelude to what has since become a keystone of UCAV doctrine, this report observed that UCAVs "provide a chance to destroy critical targets before local air superiority has been achieved and the air defenses beat down."

Even before the turn of the century, airframe designers had moved beyond the notion of simply hanging weapons on reconnaissance drones. The McDonnell Douglas (now Boeing) Phantom Works was already working on the project that would evolve into the X-45 program, the first unmanned aerial vehicle designed from the start as a combat aircraft.

On its sixth flight on December 19, 2002, the X-45A Air Vehicle 1 flew with its landing gear up for the first time. *DARPA*

On March 9, 1998, DARPA issued its document MDA972-98-R-0003, the Phase I request for proposals for an unmanned combat air vehicle advanced technology demonstrator (UCAV ATD). In conjunction with the U.S. Air Force, DARPA invited selected aircraft manufacturers to demonstrate the technical feasibility of a UCAV system that could "effectively and affordably prosecute twenty-first-century Suppression of Enemy Air Defenses (SEAD)/Strike missions within the emerging global command and control architecture."

For the first time, the word *combat* had been inserted in the UAV acronym of a project that would become a real aircraft. DARPA envisioned nothing short of a weapons system that expanded tactical mission options for "revolutionary new air power." They saw the UCAV as a weapon system that could engage multiple targets in a single mission with minimal human supervision. DARPA envisioned something that would require minimal maintenance

The Boeing X-45A Air Vehicle 1 prototype aircraft flies over the Edwards Air Force Base range in southern California on December 19, 2002. *DARPA*

Under the watchful eye of UCAV program personnel, the second Boeing X-45A prototype aircraft, Air Vehicle 2, is unloaded from an Air Reserve C-5A Galaxy after its arrival at the Dryden Flight Research Center on May 15, 2001. The shipping container seen here is similar to that in which operational UCAVs would be deployed. *DARPA*

and that could be stored for extended periods of time, unpacked, and used almost immediately in "small-scale contingencies" and major-theater wars. DARPA wanted a versatile system that could operate from an ordinary runway, conducting its missions alone, in groups, or in cooperation with manned tactical aircraft.

The UCAV was envisioned as being able to perform combat missions of a type that did not yet exist, such as high-risk tasks where the danger to human pilots was extreme, or missions where the UCAV is more cost-effective than current platforms. For instance, the initial operational role for the UCAV was seen as being that of a "first-day-of-the-war force enabler" tasked with performing the SEAD mission.

In SEAD, UCAVs would knock out the enemy air defenses before the manned bombers entered hostile air space. After accomplishing the SEAD mission, UCAVs would be used on other high-value

and/or time-critical targets. Strategically, this would present an enemy with a "no win" tactical situation in which their defenses would be ineffective. Also, DARPA noted that "advances in small smart munitions would allow these smaller vehicles to attack multiple targets during a single mission and to reduce the cost per target killed" and that "improvements in sensor technology would allow significant advances in surveillance and reconnaissance over high threat areas." As with the RQ-3 DarkStar and RQ-4 Global Hawk, DARPA wanted "intelligent function allocation" to allow the UCAV to operate *autonomously*, while stressing the idea that the human controller would be expected to provide executive-level mission management to "remain in the decision process."

A month after DARPA issued the Phase I request for proposals for the UCAV ATD, on April 16, 1998, DARPA and the Air Force made the contract awards, picking four contractors to enter the preliminary

The second Boeing X-45A prototype aircraft, minus its wings, is seen here in the hangar at the Dryden Flight Research Center after its arrival from St. Louis. The X-45A Air Vehicle 1 is seen in the background. *DARPA*

design phase. These four were Lockheed Martin Tactical Aircraft Systems, Northrop Grumman Military Aircraft Systems, Raytheon Systems, and the Boeing Company. (Over the course of the preceding two years, Boeing had acquired both McDonnell Douglas and the North American Aviation component of Rockwell International.)

As the DARPA UCAV program manager, Larry Birckelbaw, put it, Phase I had "challenged the industry teams to truly 'think out of the box' and to let the mission requirements drive them to an over-all, optimized system solution. . . . Overcoming the technical challenges to conduct these demanding and dangerous missions with an unmanned system will provide the warfighter with a revolutionary capability that saves lives." On March 24, 1999, DARPA and the Air Force selected Boeing to proceed with the 42-month second phase: the development, fabrication, and flight-testing of two demonstrator air vehicles and a reconfigurable mobile MCS.

The Air Force UCAV program manager, Lieutenant Colonel Michael Leahy, Ph.D., summarized the importance of the UCAV concept by observing that it would "exploit real-time on-board and off-board sensors for quick detection, identification and location of fixed, relocatable, and mobile targets. The system's secure communications and advanced cognitive decision aids will provide ground-based, human operators with situational awareness and positive air vehicle control necessary to authorize munitions release." Colonel Leahy added that the industry teams "pushed this concept to the limits possible in a paper study. We're very excited to take the next step." This next step would be an aircraft designated as the X-45A.

Meanwhile, on a development track several years behind that of the X-45A, both Boeing's Phantom Works and Northrop Grumman's Integrated Systems Sector (ISS) were working to develop a naval UCAV. The concept was provisionally designated as UCAV-N

The shipping container and both X-45A prototype air vehicles are emblazoned with the logos and insignia of all the agencies participating in the UCAV program. Two years later, in 2003, when the program became UCAS, the U.S. Navy insignia could be added. *DARPA*

by DARPA and the U.S. Navy. Both the mission and the control system of the UCAV-N would be like that of the UCAV, but a critical feature of the UCAV-N would be that it would be able to operate from the deck of an aircraft carrier.

Northrop Grumman moved forward with a company-funded UCAV-N prototype that it called Pegasus, and the preliminary design of this prototype was revealed in February 2001 by the company's new Advanced Systems Development Center in El Segundo, California. In June 2001, Grumman's Pegasus demonstration aircraft was officially assigned an X-prefix designation by the Department of Defense. It was planned that the demonstrator would carry the designation X-47A, and a refined UCAV-N prototype, built under the U.S. Navy/DARPA UCAV-N program, would be designated as X-47B.

Though these prototypes would lead the way into the future of twenty-first-century UCAV technology,

the United States would not be alone. In June 2003, at the biannual Paris Air Show, the French Armee de l'Air formally announced that it had selected the top French combat aircraft maker, Dassault Aviation, to develop a UCAV destined for flight-testing by 2008. Defense procurement chief Yves Gleizes said that it was a means for France to stay close to the leading edge of combat aircraft technology. It was also added that France hoped for a multination consortium to join the project to help defray costs.

Boeing X-45A

In building the X-45A, Boeing would place the management of the project under its Phantom Works component. Modeled on the Lockheed Skunk Works, Phantom Works had been created within McDonnell's St. Louis center shortly before McDonnell Douglas was acquired by Boeing in 1997. Dave Swain, the executive vice president of Phantom Works, said that his organization would

The UCAV program manager, Air Force Lieutenant Colonel Michael Leahy, Ph.D., stands with the X-45A Air Vehicle 1 at the Dryden Flight Research Center. *Bill Yenne*

draw upon "the extensive experience and resources Boeing has to offer in the areas of manned strike aircraft; weapon systems technology; unmanned air vehicles; and command, control, communications, computer, intelligence, surveillance and reconnaissance technology."

Specifically, the X-45A airframe would be a product of the former McDonnell facility at Lambert Field near St. Louis, while the mission-control system would be developed in Seattle. Additional company centers in southern California and Arizona would also be involved.

The first X-45A prototype came together slowly over 18 months, and it was officially unveiled in St. Louis in a rollout ceremony on September 27, 2000. A large audience of customers, suppliers, and employees previewed a futuristic airframe 26 feet 5 inches long, with a wingspan of 33 feet 8 inches. With no vertical tail surfaces, *height* is a misnomer in listing specifications. The fuselage is 3 feet 7 inches high at its thickest.

The X-45A weighed approximately 8,000 pounds empty, and it had the ability to carry a 3,000-pound payload in two weapons bays. For flight-test purposes, one bay would be fitted with an

Shown here is an under-the-chin close-up of the Boeing X-45A Air Vehicle 1 at the Dryden Flight Research Center. *Bill Yenne*

instrumentation pallet so that crews could have easy access to evaluate test results between flights. The other eventually would be tested as an active weapons bay.

As with existing UAVs, such as the Predator—and as was intended with future operational UCAVs—the X-45A prototype was designed to be broken down and packed in a shipping crate. This delivery-truck-size container was designed so that a half dozen would fit into the cargo hold of an Air Force C-17A Globemaster.

On November 9, 2000, Air Vehicle 1 was airlifted from St. Louis to the NASA Dryden Flight Research Center at Edwards Air Force Base in California. The second X-45A would follow on May 15, 2001. Simultaneously with the Afghanistan deployments, the Air Force was preparing for the flight-testing of the X-45A. At Dryden, low-speed taxi tests would begin on September 26, 2001, followed by the first high-speed test on March 21, 2002. The long-anticipated first flight came two months later on May 22, successfully demonstrating flight characteristics and basic operations, especially the command and control link between the X-45A and its MCS. During the 14-minute debut, the aircraft reached an air speed of 225 miles per hour and an altitude of 7,500 feet.

The X-45A Air Vehicle 2 entered the program with a first flight exactly six months later, on November 22. Color-coded in red and white to distinguish it from the blue-and-white Air Vehicle 1, it flew for a half-hour and matched the speed and altitude of its sister ship's first flight. Shortly thereafter, on December 19, the first X-45A made its first flight with its landing gear retracted. In-flight-tests of the weapons-bay doors began on February 21, 2003.

During the flight-testing, the prototypes were controlled from their mobile MCS. About the size of an average travel trailer, this facility was itself a prototype of an operational MCS. The UCAV control "trailer" was similar to those used for reconnaissance UAVs that were then in use operationally. Though the UCAV was designed to operate autonomously and was not routinely remotely controlled, a command and control link was maintained between the aircraft and a crew of two in the MCS.

The joint demonstration program began officially on April 28, 2003. These coordinated flight-tests of both X-45As were seen by DARPA as the technical heart of the program and "the key to unlocking the transformational potential of the weapon system."

This detailed close-up shows the nose probe on the Boeing X-45A Air Vehicle 1. The nose probes provide critical data during flight-test operations, but are not very "stealthy." *Bill Yenne*

Compare this close-up view of the nose probe on the Boeing X-45A Air Vehicle 2 with the previous photograph of the nose probe on its sister ship. Although vital components in flight-testing, such probes would be deleted in operational variants. *Bill Yenne*

A further milestone in exploring tactical reality with the X-45A would come on March 24, 2004, when the aircraft released an inert 250-pound bomb over the Precision Impact Range Area in the southern California desert near Edwards Air Force Base. The aircraft dropped the unguided weapon from its internal weapons bay at 35,000 feet while flying at approximately 442 miles per hour.

"What an historic day for aviation!" exclaimed George Muellner, the former Air Force general who was now the general manager of Boeing Air Force Systems. "Our team has shown the world that an autonomous unmanned combat aircraft can respond to human direction and successfully release a weapon from an internal bay. It also demonstrated the combat

Taken out of context, this photo could easily inspire some rumors of things recovered at Roswell. The Boeing X-45A air vehicle appears very much like a UFO when broken down and packed for shipping. The wings detach and slip in adjacent to the otherworldly fuselage. *Bill Yenne*

The interior of the flight operations control center (FOCC) for the X-45A is similar to that used for operations of other UAVs. From the outside, the mobile FOCC looks very much like a motor home. The man on the right is not Ron Howard. *Bill Yenne*

capability of the X-45 J-UCAS and how it will become a revolutionary force enabler capable of conducting attacks in high-threat environments." The next "strike mission" for the X-45A would be an attack using live munitions against a target at the Naval Air Warfare Center Weapons Division Range at the China Lake site in California's high desert.

Boeing X-45C

Transforming the X-45A into a weapons system was obviously the goal of the program; the two X-45A advanced technology demonstrators were intended to be followed by a full-scale X-45B test aircraft, and

finally an operational UCAV. In 2002, this latter aircraft was already being tentatively discussed under the unofficial designation A-45.

The X-45B was to have looked like a scaled-up variation of the X-45A. It was to have been larger than the X-45A—about 32 feet long and 4 feet thick, with a wingspan of 47 feet. According to the plan, the operational UCAV would have had the same dimensions as the X-45B.

Early in 2003, however, DARPA and the U.S. Air Force began to rethink this plan. Acknowledging the growing problems of access to distant, landlocked theaters, such as Afghanistan, where U.S. forces were

The Boeing X-45A Air Vehicle 1 prototype is seen here in flight with its weapons-bay door open. The vehicle's first test drop of an inert 250-pound bomb occurred on March 24, 2004, in the Precision Impact Range Area in the desert near Edwards Air Force Base. *DARPA*

then in combat, UCAV planners reconsidered. They revised the operational goals of the UCAV program for increased payload, range, and endurance. As a result of this, the X-45B was replaced by the X-45C concept, which was different from the X-45A in appearance, but about the same size as the X-45B would have been. In the course of these changes in 2003, it was imagined by the program participants that the U.S. Navy could also use the X-45C as a demonstrator platform for its UCAV-N program.

The X-45C air vehicle prototype would be built to include two full weapons bays, a stores management system, provisions for an SAR, electronic support measures (ESM), a Milstar communications-satellite interface, and aerial refueling. The avionics pallet of the X-45A would be replaced in the X-45C with a fully integrated avionics suite.

Of course, a key part of the UCAV's ability to do its job is the incorporation of low-observable stealth technology, and such considerations have been critical in the design of the X-45A and its operational progeny. As with the X-45A, there would be no vertical tail on the X-45C. Although the X-45A aircraft both had nose probes for testing purposes, the X-45C and the A-45 would be "clean." As David Lanman, deputy chief of UCAV

advanced technology demonstration at the Air Force Research Laboratory put it: "UCAV systems [must be] as low-observable as possible, to achieve their intended missions. . . . If you had a radar antenna or refueling boom projecting into the air from the surface of a UCAV, that would significantly cut down on its mandated stealthiness."

Lessons learned from the X-45A demonstration program led to a redesign of the mission-control "trailer." The system for the X-45C would incorporate updated software, as well as four, rather than two, mission-control consoles. These consoles would incorporate high-definition television (HDTV) displays.

In contrast to the X-45As, which were built solely as technology demonstrators, the X-45C aircraft would be rugged prototypes that *could* be used in operational situations. In the field, the X-45Cs and A-45s could be stored in ready-to-ship containers for years until they were needed. At that point, the UCAVs could be deployed in their containers, along with their mobile MCS. When the need arose, the container-packed UCAVs would be flown to a forward location within an 800-mile radius of the intended target. Crews would then unpack and assemble the UCAVs, a task that is intended to take

This photo illustration by Erik Simonsen is a conceptual view of a pair of operational X-45B aircraft dropping GBU-32 Joint Direct Attack Munitions (JDAM) "smart bombs" over a mountainous landscape. The U.S. Air Force *WA* tail code (which appears on the fuselage because there is no tail) identifies the base as Nellis Air Force Base in Nevada. In 2003, the Air Force chose not to build the X-45B, but to move on to the X-45C configuration. *Boeing Phantom Works*

With storm clouds gathering ominously in the distance, two Boeing X-45C unmanned combat air vehicles are heading out for a mission. *DARPA artist's concept*

just a few hours for each. Meanwhile, the MCS would be made ready, and the strike mission would be launched. As the X-45C was being planned, the Air Force envisioned that the UCAV would be deployed with gravity bombs, as well as GBU-31 and GBU-32 joint direct attack munitions (JDAM), as well as other guided air-to-surface weapons.

Northrop Grumman X-47A Pegasus

When DARPA and the U.S. Navy initiated the notion of a naval UCAV (UCAV-N) at the turn of the century, the requirement was to demonstrate the technical feasibility for a stealthy UCAV system to accomplish generally the same tasks that were planned for the Air Force UCAV. The UCAV-N would be designed to effectively conduct surveillance, strike, and SEAD missions in the twenty-first century—but to do it while operating from an aircraft carrier.

Some airframe builders went to the drawing board to come up with specific UCAV-N proposals, while Northrop Grumman's corporate management made the decision to use company funds to build an actual flying aircraft as a demonstration of their proposal for the UCAV-N. Given the name Pegasus by the company, the design concept was unveiled by Northrop Grumman's ISS in February 2001. In June of that year the aircraft was formally assigned the X-47A designation. By now, Northrop Grumman's program had received a $12 million contract from DARPA and the U.S. Navy, which would partially defray the cost of developing Pegasus.

To pursue the concept, Northrop Grumman was able to draw on its considerable recent high-technology tactical aircraft experience, including the design and development of the B-2 Spirit—the original stealth bomber—and the RQ-4 Global Hawk, which was the largest tactical reconnaissance UAV yet deployed. The company also had a substantial background in systems integration with its E-8 J-STARS aircraft, the E-2C Hawkeye airborne early-warning command and control aircraft, and its significant role in the McDonnell Douglas (now Boeing) F/A-18 Hornet and Super Hornet strike fighter aircraft.

While the Pegasus had been conceived and designed in El Segundo, California, at the air combat systems component of Northrop Grumman Integrated Systems, the actual airframe was to be built mostly of nonmetal composite materials at Scaled Composites in Mojave, California. Scaled Composites itself has an impressive pedigree, being owned and operated by the legendary Burt Rutan, the creator of numerous extraordinary aircraft, from NASA's *Proteus* high-altitude research aircraft to *Voyager*, the first—and to date, only—aircraft to circumnavigate the earth nonstop.

The official rollout of the X-47A Pegasus occurred at the Scaled Composites facility in Mojave on July 30, 2001. The kite-shaped aircraft was 27 feet 11 inches long, with a nearly equal wingspan of just under 27 feet 10 inches. With no vertical tail surfaces, the X-47A stood just 6 feet above the tarmac.

At the rollout ceremony, Scott Seymour, the vice president for Northrop Grumman's Air Combat Systems, commented that "UAVs represent a transformational capability that can cost-effectively augment manned systems. We are working closely with our customers to leverage the synergy of manned

and unmanned aircraft to accomplish current and future mission requirements." Little could he have predicted the dramatic paradigm shift in the concept of military application of UAVs that would abruptly occur as a result of events that would take place just six weeks later, on September 11.

The program moved ahead quickly, with a series of engine run tests between December 2001 and March 2002. On April 29, the Pegasus team achieved the successful autonomous start and shutdown of the aircraft's Pratt & Whitney JT15D turbofan engine. Meanwhile, the testing and integration of the avionics and software was ongoing at Northrop Grumman's Advanced Systems Development Center in El Segundo, following the same process that had been used to develop past UAVs, including the Global Hawk.

On July 19, the X-47A began a series of taxi tests at the Naval Air Warfare Center Weapons Division, located at the remote China Lake facility in California's Mojave Desert. During the taxi tests, such factors as command and control, steering, brakes, and navigation would be thoroughly scrutinized in tests that saw the X-47A taxi and stop at various points on the runway.

The first flight of the Northrop Grumman X-47A occurred on February 23, 2003, at China Lake, nine months after the debut flight of the Boeing X-45A. As fully configured for flight operations, the Pegasus weighed 3,835 pounds dry, with a total fuel capacity of 1,580 pounds. The Pratt & Whitney JT15D-5C provided 3,200 pounds of thrust.

The Pegasus successfully lifted off at 7:56 a.m. local time and touched down 12 minutes later, having been evaluated for its low-speed handling qualities, performance, and navigation. Most important, the aircraft had successfully landed near a predesignated touchdown point. This was to simulate the tail-hook capture point on an aircraft carrier flight deck, and thus to demonstrate the landing accuracy of the X-47A's "shipboard-relative" GPS, its primary navigation system. Gary Ervin of Northrop Grumman's Air Combat Systems observed later that morning, "regular unmanned flight operations aboard a flight deck at sea have never been attempted, and Pegasus addressed some of those key concerns today."

As with the Boeing X-45A, the Northrop Grumman X-47A was intended as a demonstrator aircraft that would evolve later into a tactical configuration that would look somewhat different from the A model. Just as the X-45A evolved into the X-45B

The Northrop Grumman X-47A Pegasus is seen here during its first taxi test at the Naval Air Warfare Center on July 19, 2002. It was designed to demonstrate aerodynamic qualities suitable for autonomous flight operations from an aircraft carrier as part of the UCAV-N program. *DARPA*

and the X-45C, Northrop Grumman was refining the look of its X-47A into the X-47B. This configuration was formally unveiled on April 15, 2003. The design of the X-47B would combine the kite-shaped aerodynamics of the X-47A Pegasus, but with short wings shaped rather like the outer wing sections of the Northrop B-2. As such, the kite shape was blended into a flying-wing shape that increased the overall wingspan by about a third.

As the company explained it, the kite design enabled "efficient integration of propulsion and weapons, while the wing extensions provide aerodynamic efficiency." The new design would also provide the tactical variant with longer endurance, as well as "high survivability and the low-speed, aerodynamic flying qualities for precision landing and autonomous launch and recovery operations" from an aircraft carrier.

Two weeks after the X-47B's unveiling, on May 1st 2003, DARPA formally approved the vehicle's configuration and awarded Northrop Grumman a contract worth up to $160 million to produce and demonstrate two full-scale X-47B UCAVs. The formal approval of the X-47B coincided with DARPA's decision to merge the X-45 UCAV program and the

X-47 UCAV-N program into the single joint project under its new Joint Unmanned Combat Air Systems office discussed below.

Joint Unmanned Combat Air Systems

Though the actual office would not be formally opened until the first of October 2003, DARPA officially created its joint unmanned combat air systems (J-UCAS) department on April 28, 2003. Located with DARPA's other offices in Arlington, Virginia, the new (J-UCAS) office would be staffed by representatives from DARPA, as well as both the Air Force and the Navy.

The idea of J-UCAS was to bring both the X-45, which was primarily a U.S. Air Force program, and the X-47, mainly a U.S. Navy project, under the same umbrella. Both programs had a great deal in common. They were generally in the same size and weight class, and both were designed to be autonomous, unmanned, stealth-attack aircraft, albeit for separate military services.

Previously, the two separate programs had been specifically targeted toward their service-specific needs, but the Defense Department now recognized the potential for "significant synergy" by combining them. Of course, a major reason for the change was cost reduction, which is always a concern within the Department of Defense when new programs are in their gestation phase.

J-UCAS specifically sought to reduce acquisition costs, as well as operation and support costs. At the time J-UCAS was created, DARPA noted the various features that the two programs had in common—but which were distinct from other combat aircraft. "Removing the pilot from the vehicle eliminates man-rating requirements, pilot systems, and interfaces," DARPA reported. "New design philosophies can be used to optimize the design for aerodynamics, signature, reduced maintenance and low cost manufacturing processes."

Moving forward, both second-generation UCAVs, the X-45C and the X-47B, would have to accommodate new science and technology requirements that would be common to both the Navy and Air Force. These shared objectives would now include a combat radius of 1,500 miles, with a payload of 4,500 pounds and the ability of the UCAV to loiter for two hours over a target up to 1,100 miles from the takeoff point.

The mission package remained the same—"the dull, the dirty, and the dangerous"—although not necessarily in that order. The "dangerous," the SEAD mission, was still foremost, followed by the capability to conduct immediate lethal strikes against high-value, highly protected, and time-critical targets. The "dirty" missions would still include strikes against chemical or biological weapons sites. Finally, the UCAVs could fly the "dull" and repetitive reconnaissance missions, such as enforcing "no-fly" zones.

As previously conceived under the earlier, separate programs, the J-UCAS program would continue to be conducted in "multiple overlapping spirals" of increasing capability that moved toward the objective system. The first such spiral was designated *Spiral Zero*, and was not to be confused with the earlier Spiral Zero evaluation that the X-45A had undertaken. The new Spiral Zero would involve the two existing X-45As and a single X-47A demonstrator aircraft, along with all their associated simulation, mission-control, and support systems. The succeeding Spiral One would involve evaluation of the stealthy X-45C and X-47B full-scale demonstrators. These were envisioned as being generally in the same size and configuration as the ultimate tactical aircraft, which were informally referred to as "A-45" and "A-47." The X-45C and X-47B and their associated

The debut flight of the Northrop Grumman X-47A Pegasus occurred on February 23, 2003, at the Naval Air Warfare Center at China Lake, California. *Northrop Grumman Media Relations*

The Northrop Grumman X-47A Pegasus took off on its first flight at 7:56 on the morning of February 23, 2003, flew for 12 minutes, and then landed near a predesignated touchdown point. *Northrop Grumman Media Relations*

mission-control equipment would certainly be capable of demonstrating the payload, performance, and range of the final tactical configurations. By the second decade of the twenty-first century, the once-unbelievable notion of an operational UCAV would be a reality.

Crews move an operational UCAV-N into takeoff position on the deck of an aircraft carrier in this 2003 Northrop Grumman composite photo illustration. This configuration would enable long endurance and high survivability with excellent carrier launch and recovery flying qualities. *Northrop Grumman Media Relations*

UCAV Helicopters

The idea of a rotary-wing aerial vehicle has always been attractive to combat commanders. Helicopters can take off vertically and land vertically—on virtually any surface—without the need for a runway. Just as manned helicopters helped to revolutionize battlefields and battlefield tactics in Korea and Vietnam, unmanned and autonomous helicopters have the potential of changing the way air operations are conducted in the twenty-first century.

When the U.S. Navy began evaluating the Northrop Grumman Fire Scout under its vertical take-off and landing tactical unmanned aerial vehicle (VTUAV) program in 2000, it was seen as a platform for reconnaissance and targeting support. Within a few years, as armed, fixed-wing drones were proving their high value in Afghanistan and Iraq, plans were laid to arm the Fire Scout as well.

Meanwhile, the Boeing X-50A Dragonfly was being developed as an evaluation platform for future vertical takeoff and landing attack aircraft that would be capable of cruising to their targets at high-subsonic speeds. Such aircraft would make it possible to penetrate hostile enemy territory at low altitudes and high speeds. As with fixed-wing UCAVs, the rotary-wing descendents of the X-50A would be able to strike targets without risking their pilots.

RQ-8A Fire Scout

The Northrop Grumman Fire Scout originated in 2000 as the U.S. Navy's VTUAV program. It is a twenty-first-century rotary-wing tactical UAV that is designed for autonomous operations from confined spaces that require vertical takeoffs and landings. It was designed to be capable of operating autonomously from the deck of smaller warships, such as destroyers, as well as amphibious ships and cruisers.

Under VTUAV, the U.S. Navy envisioned the Fire Scout drone helicopter as being capable of providing reconnaissance and precision-targeting support for its ships at sea and for Marine Corps forces ashore. It was only after the success of the armed Predator in Afghanistan that the Navy decided that the Fire Scout should also carry offensive weapons.

The Navy originally intended that the VTUAV vehicle would eventually replace the RQ-2 Pioneer reconnaissance UAV. The Pioneer needed a runway or an elaborate shipboard launch and recovery system, while the VTUAV would not. As Northrop Grumman put it, "The small footprint of the VTUAV would reduce the impact on flight deck operations compared to the Pioneer, resulting in a major paradigm shift on tactical UAV operations.

In February 2000, Northrop Grumman was awarded a $93 million cost-plus-incentive contract for the engineering and manufacturing development phase of the VTUAV project. For its money, the Navy would receive one "system" of three vehicles, as well as technical manuals, operations security, operational and maintenance training, and technical support prior to the vehicle becoming operational.

The specific mandate of the VTUAV program was to create a long-endurance vehicle with a continuous surveillance capability of more than six hours, and an operational radius of 126 miles. The sensor package would include electro-optical/infrared systems, as well as a laser target designator. The designator would be a great "force multiplier" for ships equipped with extended range guided munitions (ERGMs), firing 5-inch guns or land-attack missiles. The VTUAV should also be able to conduct real-time battle-damage assessment.

Meanwhile, additional "mission areas for future growth payloads" included mine countermeasures, battle management, chemical and biological weapons reconnaissance, signals intelligence, electronic warfare, combat search and rescue, communications and data relay, information warfare, ship missile defense, and antisubmarine warfare.

While Northrop Grumman Corporation's Ryan Aeronautical Center in San Diego is the lead contractor for the Fire Scout program, the aerial vehicle itself is based on the Schweizer Aircraft Corporation Model 300-series manned turbine helicopter, which had previously been proven by over 20 million flight hours. To develop the vehicle, Northrop Grumman brought together a team of subcontractors. In addition to Schweizer Aircraft, which would build the airframe in Elmira, New York, the team also included Lockheed Martin Federal Systems of Oswego, New

York, and L-3 Communications of Salt Lake City. The sensor payload would be developed by Northrop Grumman Electronic Sensors and Systems Sector based in Baltimore, along with TAMAM-Israel Aircraft Industries.

The first several Fire Scout test airframes were delivered to Northrop Grumman by Schweizer during the summer of 2001. These airframes were 22 feet 11 inches long, with a rotor diameter of 27 feet 6 inches. When fully fitted out for flight operations, each would weigh 3,150 pounds and would have a payload capacity of up to 300 pounds. In terms of performance, the Fire Scout would have a top speed in excess of 140 miles per hour and a service ceiling of 20,000 feet.

The first flight of an unmanned Fire Scout VTUAV, officially designated as RQ-8A, occurred at dawn on May 19, 2002, at the Naval Air Systems Command Western Test Range Complex at China Lake in California. During the course of this flight, the RQ-8A took off autonomously and climbed to an altitude of 30 feet. From there, it made the transition to forward flight while continuing the climb to more than 200 feet. The flight executed by the Fire Scout consisted of a series of course changes at preprogrammed waypoints. The RQ-8A then autonomously landed and shut itself down. As the

This cutaway illustration shows the internal structure, engine, and payload component details of the RQ-8A Fire Scout. *Northrop Grumman Media Relations*

An RQ-8A Fire Scout is shown here in August 2003 aboard the amphibious transport dock ship USS *Denver* (LPD-9) with its engine running and rotors engaged. In two months of shipboard suitability and flight testing, the aircraft conducted over 80 sorties totaling more than 65 flight hours. *Northrop Grumman Media Relations*

This production-configured RQ-8A Fire Scout was fitted with an all-weather, high-resolution, tactical synthetic-aperture radar/moving-target indicator (SAR/MTI) payload package. Northrop Grumman undertook the integration and end-to-end air vehicle/payload testing of this Fire Scout as a demonstration for the U.K. Ministry of Defence's Watchkeeper program. *Northrop Grumman Media Relations*

flight-test program unfolded, the Fire Scout gradually demonstrated greater range and altitude capability. The original six-hour endurance requirement would be met and exceeded by an additional two hours.

As the RQ-8A entered its low-rate initial production phase in 2002, the plan was to deploy the first system with the U.S. Marine Corps. In addition to three Fire Scout aircraft, the introductory system would include two ground-control stations, data links, remote data terminals, modular mission payloads, launch and recovery equipment, and tactical communications equipment. Eventually, the RQ-8A systems would be configured to include four Fire Scout aircraft.

Original testing of the Fire Scout aboard a ship

was conducted during the latter part of 2003 using the USS *Denver* (LPD-9). Initially, a Fire Scout vehicle and its ground-control station operated from the ship in San Diego harbor, and then from the ship as it got under way along the Pacific Coast between San Diego and Naval Base Ventura County at Point Mugu. Among the tests conducted was using the ground-control station to remotely control engine starts "ship to shore" and "shore to ship" at distances exceeding 10 miles. Other operations included deck handling and testing for electromagnetic interference and data-link connections.

Though the Fire Scout was originally developed for the U.S. Navy and Marine Corps, in January 2004 the U.S. Army embraced it as part of that service's Future Combat System program. The Army awarded Northrop Grumman a $115 million contract to develop a Fire Scout variation as the Class IV unmanned aerial system (UAS) under the designation RQ-8B. The Army saw this vehicle as a key element of tactical intelligence, surveillance, reconnaissance, and targeting at the brigade level. The RQ-8B vehicles would be similar to the RQ-8A Fire Scouts being produced for the Navy, but they would have a four-blade, rather than a three-blade, rotor. This system used an improved airfoil rotor blade to enhance performance and increase payload capacity to 600 pounds.

The Navy and Marine Corps had announced a requirement for 73 Fire Scouts, while the Army said that they might be interested in another 180. The U.S. Homeland Security Department had projected a possible acquisition of 99 aircraft, most of which would go to the U.S. Coast Guard.

Beginning in 2004, the U.K. Ministry of Defence also evaluated the Fire Scout for its Watchkeeper UAV battlefield imagery and intelligence program. Watchkeeper was intended to develop the ultimate replacement for the British-built Phoenix fixed-wing UAV. For the Watchkeeper trials, Northrop Grumman incorporated a General Atomics Lynx all-weather, high-resolution, tactical synthetic-aperture radar and moving-target indicator (SAR/MTI) on the company's production-configured Fire Scout demonstrator. Other equipment installed aboard the Fire Scout for the Watchkeeper program included a General Atomics AN/APY-8 gimbaled antenna assembly, a radar electronics assembly, and an independent GPS. Tests of this configuration were conducted at Naval Air Station Patuxent River in Maryland.

Both the RQ-8A and RQ-8B were being engineered for the installation of two four-packs of

Nicknamed *Dragonfly*, the X-50A rolled out at Boeing's rotorcraft facility at Mesa, Arizona, in 2001. The first flight would occur two years later across that state at the U.S. Army's Proving Ground near Yuma. *Boeing Phantom Works*

2.75-inch rocket launchers designed to fire the Advanced Precision Kill Weapon System laser-guided rockets. Plans were also afoot to arm the Fire Scouts with the Viper Strike laser-guided precision munition.

X-50A Dragonfly

In May 1998, Boeing and DARPA agreed to equally share the cost of developing an unmanned rotary-wing, high-speed, VTOL aircraft. Originally known as the Canard Rotor/Wing (CRW) after the Boeing-patented design concept on which it is based, the aircraft was subsequently given the designation X-50A.

The X-50A combines the hover efficiency and low-speed flight characteristics of a helicopter with the high-subsonic cruising speed of a fixed-wing aircraft. Powered by a conventional turbofan engine in both rotary-wing and fixed-wing flight, an X-50A would be able to take off and land within confined areas—such as the deck of a small ship—and to transition quickly to and from a fixed-wing mode. Seventeen feet 8 inches long, and 6 feet 6 inches high, the X-50A has twin rotors with a diameter of 12 feet.

The idea of an aircraft that could take off and land vertically while transitioning to airplanelike forward flight was not new. It was flight-tested in a manned aircraft during the late 1970s with Bell's V-15 research aircraft. This project, in turn, led to the manned V-22 Osprey tactical transport, a cooperative effort between Bell and Boeing that debuted in 1989. The concept was also incorporated into the Boeing Heliwing and the Bell Eagle Eye experimental UAV programs that are discussed earlier in this volume.

Unlike the V-22, which uses a mechanical drivetrain and transmission, the X-50A would use diverter valves to direct the thrust from a conventional turbofan engine alternately to the rotor blade tips, or aft to a jet nozzle. A dual-bleed thrust would be used during the transition phase. By using the reaction-drive rotor system, the CRW design fully eliminated the need for a mechanical drivetrain and transmission, as well as the need for an antitorque system. Eliminating these typically heavy, maintenance-intensive systems would greatly reduce vehicle weight, maintenance, and complexity, as well as cost.

Known familiarly as the "Dragonfly," the X-50A was designed by Boeing's Phantom Works component, the advanced research and development unit that was created within the company and tasked with providing advanced solutions and breakthrough technologies. The actual X-50A airframe was built at the helicopter development and manufacturing facility in Mesa, Arizona, that was once Hughes Helicopters. Acquired by McDon-nell Douglas in 1984, the site became part of Boeing in 1997. The best-known product manufactured at Mesa is the AH-64 Apache series of attack helicopters. In addition to their strong background in helicopters, the companies that have been part of Boeing since 1997 also have specific expertise in previous work on reaction-drive rotor systems, including both the XH-17 in the early 1950s and the XV-9A in the mid-1960s.

Rolled out in Mesa in 2001, the X-50A made its first flight on the morning of December 4, 2003, at the U.S. Army Proving Ground near Yuma, Arizona. The flight-test program experienced a serious setback four months later, when the first of two X-50As was damaged in a mishap at Yuma on March 23, 2004. The second test vehicle remained on standby at Mesa to be moved to Yuma to continue the flight-testing.

Ultimately, the military potential for the X-50A, or an aircraft like it, is extensive. The U.S. Navy and Marine Corps, as well as the Army, had expressed interest in the CRW concept. Missions such as reconnaissance, communications, data relay, and logistical resupply were considered, as were armed combat operations in high-risk areas such as urban terrain. The Navy and Marines found the ability of a CRW aircraft to operate from a small helicopter pad on a ship especially attractive.

Indeed, a tactical follow-on to the X-50A could fulfill the missions addressed by helicopters or complement those flown by the V-22 Osprey. These might range from reconnaissance and logistical transport to tactical air support. The Dragonfly is also seen as a potential armed escort for the Osprey on missions requiring deep penetration into hostile enemy territory.

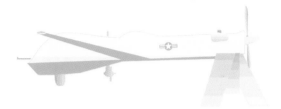

Epilogue

The idea of the combat-configured UAV, the UCAV, entered the twenty-first century much as the idea of military airplanes had entered the twentieth century—as an untried and untested concept that would soon and suddenly be thrust into the spotlight in an unexpected global war. Just as most military commanders in the first decade of the twentieth century had a hard time imagining how to use airplanes, so too did most military commanders at the end of that century have a hard time seeing UAVs as anything more than an observation platform. When the world celebrated the end of the millennium on the last day of 1999, few people outside the armed forces of a handful of countries had recognized the potential of armed, unmanned flying vehicles. For decades, even most military pilots had resisted the idea.

In 1916, the United States fought its first war that would routinely involve airplanes. General John J. "Blackjack" Pershing led an unsuccessful expedition into Mexico to track down the bandito-turned-terrorist, Francisco "Pancho" Villa. Villa's attack against civilians in the town of Columbus, New Mexico, was a small-scale analogue to what would

LEFT: *In this dramatic sunrise view, the U.S. Navy's RQ-8A Fire Scout vertical takeoff and landing (VTOL) tactical UAV greets another day of developmental flight-tests in October 2003. The location is the Webster Field Annex at Naval Air Station Patuxent River in Maryland. U.S. Navy—Kurt Lengfield*

happen to New York and Washington, D.C. 85 years later. In the course of the 1916 operation, rickety Curtiss JN-2 observation planes were pressed into service. Factors ranging from weather to high-elevation terrain resulted in the aircraft being hard to use and of marginal utility. A year later, American military aircraft were proving themselves in the skies over the western front of World War I.

Fast-forward to the last days of the twentieth century. Operation Allied Force had just concluded, and virtually the same derogatory epithets that had been said of the JN-2s in Mexico were being said of the performance of the RQ-1 Predators in the Balkans. Suddenly, the United States was at war, the enemy was in the crosshairs of an unarmed observation drone, and the cry went out to "arm the Predator!"

Even before Qaed Senyan al-Harthi and Kamal Derwish were taken out in Yemen in 2002, the notion of an armed drone fighting the evil gangsters of the world had captured the imagination of the world. Within the space of a very few months, armed drones were in action over the deserts of the Middle East, and the next generation of stealth UCAVs were making their debut flights from airfields in the high desert of California.

Just as it had been a century earlier with military airplanes themselves, armed drones had quickly made a name for themselves. They had earned a permanent place for themselves on the battlefields of the twenty-first century.

About the Author

Bill Yenne is the San Francisco–based author of more than two dozen books on military, aviation, and historical topics. He is also a member of the American Aviation Historical Society and the American Book Producers Association, as well as a graduate of the Stanford Professional Publishing Course.

He is a regular contributor to *World Air Power Review* and has written extensively about aviation and aerospace history, including corporate histories of most of the major American aircraft manufacturers: Boeing, Convair, Lockheed, McDonnell Douglas, North American, and Rockwell International. Jack Hilliard, Curator of the U.S. Air Force Museum, has called Mr. Yenne's aviation books "not only visually attractive, but very useful in day to day museum work."

Other works include *ACES: True Stories of Victory & Valor in the Skies over World War II*, *Secret Weapons of World War II*, and *SAC: A Primer of Strategic Air Power*. Of the latter, Major Michael Perini wrote in *Air Force Magazine*: "This book deserves a place on any airman's bookshelf and in the stacks of serious military libraries."

Mr. Yenne is also the author of *100 Events That Shaped World History*, about which the Texas USA network said: "If you are a student of history, you are going to want this book. If you are *not* a student of history, you are going to *need* this book."

Mr. Yenne was also a contributor and aviation consultant to *The Simon & Schuster D-Day Encyclopedia*. He worked with legendary U.S. Air Force commander General Curtis E. LeMay to produce *Superfortress: The B-29 and American Airpower in World War II*, which *Publisher's Weekly* described as "eloquent."

Index

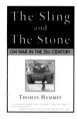

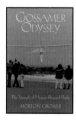

ATTACK
of the
DRONES
A History of Unmanned Aerial Combat

Bill Yenne

ZENITH
PRESS

First published in 2004 by Zenith Press, an imprint of
MBI Publishing Company, Galtier Plaza, Suite 200,
380 Jackson Street, St. Paul, MN 55101-3885 USA

Zenith Press titles are also available at discounts in bulk
quantity for industrial or sales-promotional use. For details
write to Special Sales Manager at Motorbooks International
Wholesalers & Distributors, Galtier Plaza, Suite 200, 380
Jackson Street, St. Paul, MN 55101-3885 USA.

ISBN 0-7603-1825-5

On the cover, main: A MQ-1 Predator hunts for an elusive
prey. The Predator became the symbol of a paradigm shift
in battlefield tactics that put unmanned aerial vehicles on
the attack. *Erik Simonsen.* **Bottom left:** The future of
unmanned combat air vehicles in the twenty-first century is
summarized in this artist's conception of an air strike being
conducted by a pair of Northrop Grumman quiet
supersonic platform (QSP) vehicles. This is the combat
version of an aircraft developed by the company in
cooperation with the U.S. DARPA's Quiet Supersonic
Platform program. *Northrop Grumman Media Relations*
Bottom right: The Boeing X-45A Air Vehicle 1 prototype
aircraft flies over the Edwards Air Force Base range in
southern California on December 19, 2002. *DARPA*

On the frontispiece: The Boeing X-45A, undergoing an
engine checkout at the 2001 Dryden Flight Research
Center, is the first prototype of an unmanned combat air
vehicle that was built from the ground up as a warplane
without a pilot aboard. *DARPA photo*
On the title page: The first Boeing YQM-94A awaits its
flight on the Compass Cope program, the initial effort by
the U.S. Air Force to develop a high-flying, long-endurance
reconnaissance drone. *U.S. Air Force*

On the table of contents, main: The Northrop Grumman
X-47A Pegasus summarizes a new genre of warplanes that
made its debut at the dawn of the twenty-first century.
Northrop Grumman via DARPA. **Top left:** The Canadair
CL-227 Sentinel is being tested aboard a ship at sea.
Powered by a Williams WTS34 engine, it stood 54 inches
high and was evaluated by the Canada and United States
military services. *Author's collection*. **Top middle:** These
Grumman RQ-4A Global Hawks are ready to fly, and their
high-altitude missions may keep them aloft through another
sunrise or two. Their long endurance could take them
halfway around the world before they rest and refuel.
Northrop Grumman photo. **Top right:** A twenty-first-century
naval unmanned combat air vehicle (UCAV-N) touches
down on the deck of an aircraft carrier. The aircrafts'
configuration enables long endurance, high survivability,
and excellent carrier launch and recovery flying qualities.
Northrop Grumman Media Relations photo

On the back cover, bottom left: Seen here over the USS
Tarawa amphibious assault ship in November 1997 is a
General Atomics Gnat-750, the precursor to the Predator.
The "pilot" is aboard the ship. *General Atomics Aeronautical
Systems*. **Bottom right:** The Predator is on patrol, armed
with an AGM-114 Hellfire missile. The tail code identifies it
as being based at Nellis Air Force Base, while the insignia on
the forward fuselage is that of the 11th Reconnaissance
Squadron. *General Atomics Aeronautical Systems*. **Top:**
Operational X-45B aircrafts are dropping GBU-32 Joint
Direct Attack Munitions (JDAM) "smart bombs" over a
mountainous landscape. In 2003 the Air Force chose not to
build the X-45B, but to move on to the X-45C
configuration. *Erik Simonsen via Boeing Phantom Works*

Edited by Steve Gansen
Designed by Katie Sonmor

Printed in China